TRANSFORMING GIRLS

Children's Literature Association Series

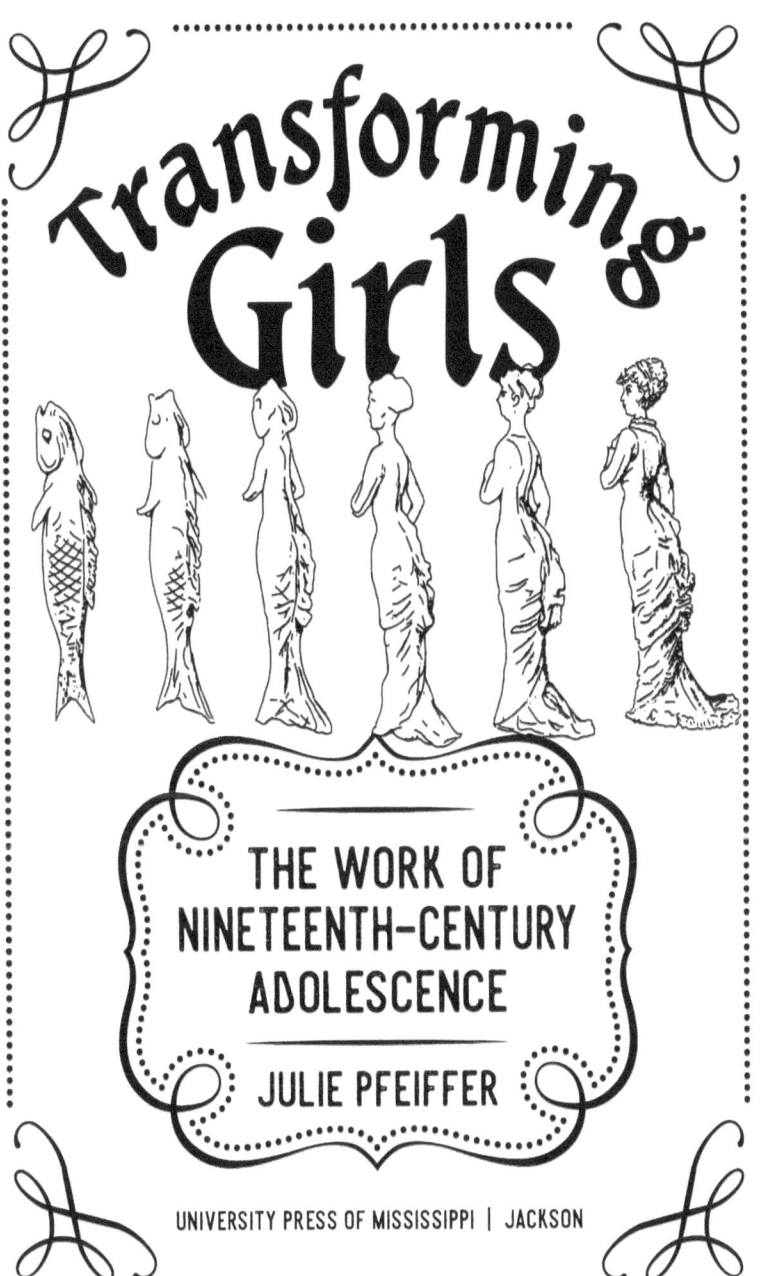

Transforming Girls

THE WORK OF NINETEENTH-CENTURY ADOLESCENCE

JULIE PFEIFFER

UNIVERSITY PRESS OF MISSISSIPPI | JACKSON

The University Press of Mississippi is the scholarly publishing agency of
the Mississippi Institutions of Higher Learning: Alcorn State University,
Delta State University, Jackson State University, Mississippi State University,
Mississippi University for Women, Mississippi Valley State University,
University of Mississippi, and University of Southern Mississippi.

www.upress.state.ms.us

The University Press of Mississippi is a member
of the Association of University Presses.

Copyright © 2021 by Julie Pfeiffer
All rights reserved
Manufactured in the United States of America

Material in *Transforming Girls: The Work of Nineteenth-Century Adolescence*
(Pfeiffer) appeared in altered form in these publications:
"The Backfisch and Stories of Female Adolescence." *Tulsa Studies in
Women's Literature* 36, no. 2 (Fall 2017): 295–321.
"The Romance of Othermothering in Nineteenth-Century Backfisch Books."
In *Mothers in Children's and Young Adult Literature: From the Eighteenth Century
to Postfeminism*, edited by Lisa Rowe Fraustino and Karen Coats, 59–74. Jackson:
University Press of Mississippi, 2016.

First printing 2021
∞

Library of Congress Cataloging-in-Publication Data

Names: Pfeiffer, Julie (Julie Kristine), author.
Title: Transforming girls : the work of nineteenth-century adolescence /
Julie Pfeiffer.
Other titles: Children's Literature Association series.
Description: Jackson : University Press of Mississippi, 2021. | Series:
Children's literature association series | Includes bibliographical
references and index.
Identifiers: LCCN 2021031170 (print) | LCCN 2021031171 (ebook) | ISBN
9781496836267 (hardback) | ISBN 9781496836274 (trade paperback) | ISBN
9781496836281 (epub) | ISBN 9781496836298 (epub) | ISBN 9781496836304
(pdf) | ISBN 9781496836311 (pdf)
Subjects: LCSH: Girls in literature. | Adolescence in literature. | Teenage
girls in literature. | Young adult fiction, American—History and
criticism. | Young adult fiction, German—History and criticism. |
American literature—19th century—History and criticism. | German
literature—19th century—History and criticism.
Classification: LCC PN56.5.A35 P45 2021 (print) | LCC PN56.5.A35 (ebook)
| DDC 809./.93352352—dc23
LC record available at https://lccn.loc.gov/2021031170
LC ebook record available at https://lccn.loc.gov/2021031171

British Library Cataloging-in-Publication Data available

For my parents

Contents

ix   Acknowledgments

3   INTRODUCTION

41   CHAPTER ONE • Defining the Backfisch

65   CHAPTER TWO • The Romance of Othermothering

93   CHAPTER THREE • Converting Girls into Women

117   CHAPTER FOUR • The Backfisch and Fantasies of Growth

141   CHAPTER FIVE • The Homesick Heroine

165   CONCLUSION • Loving Girls, Loving Growth

171   Notes

179   Works cited

191   Index

Acknowledgments

I am grateful for this chance to thank some of the people and institutions who supported me financially, intellectually, and emotionally through the long process of writing this book.

It began with the women who taught me reading is a pleasure and handed me books they loved—Margaret Aldrich, Carol Pfeiffer, and Peggy Kidwell; with my father, who shared his love of language and travel; with my sisters, Carin-Anna Pfeiffer and Shaili Pfeiffer, who remind me constantly of the power of female community; and with Bianca Bielig Mencocco, who taught me to dream in German.

It also began with the professors who helped me to see that texts tell multiple stories, especially Owen Jenkins, Jean Marsden, Regina Barecca, and Myra Marx Ferree. This project would not have been imagined without colleagues, including Hans-Heino Ewers, U. C. Knoepflmacher, J. D. Stahl, Lee Talley, and Roberta Seelinger Trites, whose generous sharing of materials, ideas, and encouragement helped me to ask new questions.

I have been supported in ways too numerous to name comprehensively. I relied on the financial support of Hollins University, the Fulbright Scholar Program, the German Academic Exchange Service, and the Berry Professorship in Liberal Studies. I am also indebted to the librarians at the Institut für Jugendbuchforschung, Penn State, the New York Public Library, the Staatsbibliothek zu Berlin, and especially Hollins University. I benefited tremendously from the work of editors who helped me refine my writing process, ideas, and prose, including Anne Amienne, Karen Coats, Karen Dutoi, Elizabeth Farry, Lisa Rowe Fraustino, Mary Heath, Katie Keene, Laura Stevens, Ellen Tilton-Cantrell, and Audra Wolfe. Portions of this work appeared in earlier forms in *Tulsa Studies in Women's Literature* and *Mothers in Children's and Young Adult Literature: From the Eighteenth Century to Postfeminism*. I am especially appreciative of the anonymous reviewers whose encouragement and questions pushed me to expand and clarify my argument and the many students who inspired and challenged me. Special thanks to Marissa Bolin and Abigail Parks, who helped with research and editing.

This project would not have been finished without the friends and colleagues whose generous reading, encouragement, and support were crucial to the development of my ideas and my sense of joy in writing, including Deann Bishop, Amanda Cockrell, LeeRay Costa, Jennifer Deegan, Michelle De Groot, Christine Doyle, Amy Gerber-Stroh, Elisabeth Gruner, Lori Joseph, Pauline Kaldas, Elizabeth Keyser, Gina Kohler, Jeanne Larsen, Julia McQuillan, Phil Nel, Kathleen Nolan, Rachel Nuñez, Anne Phillips, Lisa Radcliff, Darla Schumm, Rebecca Seipp, Robin Taylor, Sam Thayer, and Jill Weber.

I was sustained in this work by the many family members who saw me as a writer first even when there were dishes to be done or family gatherings to plan, especially my son Jack, whose nightly question, "Have you written today?" kept this book alive.

TRANSFORMING GIRLS

Introduction

In chapter 2 of Dorothy Canfield's 1916 novel *Understood Betsy*, Betsy arrives at her cousins' Vermont cabin in distress. An anxious city child, Betsy is in shock at losing her caregivers and overwhelmed by an unfamiliar world. Betsy is particularly distraught to learn she will share a bed with Aunt Abigail; she has been sternly inculcated with the belief that it is "bad for children to sleep with grown-ups." In a "strange, ugly little room" with a "strange, queer, fat old woman," Betsy feels utterly bereft. But as Betsy lies in bed and watches her Aunt Abigail read Emerson's essays, her shock turns to pleasure as the "rampart of Aunt Abigail's great body" allows her to let go of the cold night and her fears.

In my own childhood, the stories of Betsy, Anne, Rebecca, Heidi, and Jo let me rest in the security of familiar narratives, as relaxing as the warmth of my mother's body next to me as I fell asleep. Later, in courses in feminist literary criticism, I wondered about that comfort. Had I been seduced by the lure of a gender regime that promised me that being a good girl—domestic, obedient, quiet—would keep the dark shadows at bay, would keep me safe? Why, I wondered, did I love these books that so clearly asked girls to give up ambition for community, that were complicit (as Estes and Lant so provocatively argue[1]) in the murder of *Little Women*'s Jo?

The answer I will propose here came not from reading the girls' books that enveloped me as a child and still comfort me now, but from discovering another world of girls' books, the popular German girls' books of the mid-nineteenth century. I had been reading girls' books for thirty years, and studying them for fifteen, when a colleague handed me a stack of German girls' books, unknown, and yet familiar. Gretchen, Ilse, Lenore, Henny—new names to add to an inner landscape of girls who had taught me the path to happiness lies in domestic order. As I studied these books, and was led by them to unfamiliar mid-nineteenth-century American girls' books, I discovered some key differences. Unlike family stories such as Louisa May Alcott's *Little Women* (1868) or Charlotte Yonge's *The Daisy Chain* (1856), these books were about journeys from home. And unlike the orphan girls—Sarah Crewe, Anne, Pollyanna—these girls had parents and siblings. Most significantly, the new texts I discovered focused not on the girl child, but on the adolescent girl. They deliberately, evocatively, called up an experience of transition and marked that experience as significant.

This project explores the paradox of the nineteenth-century girls' book: it relies on gender binaries and suggests girls must accommodate and support a patriarchal framework to be happy. It also provides access to imagined worlds centered on adolescent girls. The early girls' book frames female adolescence as an opportunity, a space of productive investment in the self. This is a space where mentors who trust themselves, the education they provide, and the girl's essentially good nature neutralize the protagonist's own anxieties about maturing. These mid-nineteenth-century novels focus on female adolescence as a social category in ways that are unexpected to contemporary readers. They rely not on twentieth-century models of the alienated adolescent but on a model of collaborative growth. They help us approach adolescence—a category that continues to engage and perplex us—from another perspective, one that celebrates fluid identity and the deliberate construction of a self. They provide alternatives to contemporary cultural beliefs about what it was like to be a girl in the nineteenth century, and challenge the assumption that the evolution of the girls' book is always a movement toward less sexist, less restrictive images of girls. In the chapters that follow, I lay out the qualities of nineteenth-century adolescent girls' fiction and ask what its vision of transformative work can offer contemporary girls and the adults who care about them.

Reading the Girls' Book

There's a conversation I have, usually with other women whose mothers or grandmothers or aunts handed them books with worn covers and said, "I think you'll like this one." Sometimes it's a conversation I have with men, as when a dear friend said, "Of course I've read *Little Women*; my mother insisted." It's a moment of connection, of finding out we know the same people, spent summers in the same fictional worlds of girls who felt closer at times than the real people who populated our lives. When I talk with these people, it's as if we grew up together, shared domestic misadventures, despite differences of age and geography and family situation. We can tell the story of Anne's intoxication of Diana more readily than the story of our own eighth birthday parties; we filter our own anger through the image of Marmee's tight lips.

Perhaps because the girls' book has such a powerful influence on so many lives, it has been the subject of extensive critical study.[2] Critics agree it is difficult to untangle what writers meant by "the girl" in the nineteenth century; the term often conflates childhood, adolescence, and young womanhood. While the word "girl" in the world of girls' fiction has different meanings according to time period, class, race, and nationality, it usually refers to unmarried female-identified individuals under the age of twenty. The girls' book is a subcategory of children's literature, typically defined as books written with girls as an intended audience (as opposed to a more general category of books read by girls).[3] The genre can include books used in schools or religious settings as well as books intended for the girls' entertainment. While critics typically see the girls' book as emerging in the eighteenth century, some critics argue for an earlier origin. Cornelia Niekus Moore, for example, discusses earlier books written for German girls in her book *The Maiden's Mirror: Reading Material for German Girls in the Sixteenth and Seventeenth Centuries*. The genre as we see it today, in the form of popular books for the entertainment of girls, exploded in the second half of the nineteenth century, when realistic fiction for middle-class girls became an important category in the literary marketplace in both Europe and North America.

This fiction appeared both as novels for girls and in early periodicals such as *Merry's Museum, Godey's Lady's Book*, and *Die Gartenlaube: Illustriertes Familienblatt* (*The Garden Bower: An Illustrated Magazine for Families*). It reflects both social and technological shifts in Western countries in the nineteenth century: a developing concept of children as innocent and deserving of entertainment; higher literacy rates; an accumulation of wealth, which meant some girls had more leisure time; the association of reading with upward social mobility; the opening of public libraries in some communities; cheaper printing; and increased avenues of distribution.⁴ In nineteenth-century America—where laws against teaching enslaved people to read and write existed in some southern states, and Black children were not permitted access to public education in many northern communities—the market for these publications was assumed to be white, middle-class girls whose families could afford a period of leisure time for their daughters before marriage.⁵ Racial identity was linked to religion and language in nineteenth-century Germany (relevant debates centered on the place of Jews or Poles in Germany, for example); the German Backfisch book typically assumes a white, Protestant, upper-middle-class girl as its protagonist. In both Germany and the United States, writing for girls was further constrained by geography; the authors and assumed readers of novels for girls were more likely to be from the north than the south (Prussians, in Germany; New Englanders, in the United States).

In both countries, one of the qualities of the early novel for girls is a hidden focus on whiteness as an identity linked to femininity and moral virtue. Cultural historian Robin Bernstein argues for the ways "childhood innocence—itself raced white, itself characterized by the ability to retain racial meanings but hide them under claims of holy obliviousness—secured the unmarked status of whiteness" in nineteenth-century America (8). Girls' books suggest white girls are protected by their behavior, not their skin color; a focus on domesticity and the leisure time for cultural development are defined as qualities of character rather than circumstance. As Nazera Sadiq Wright points out, "The 'prematurely knowing' black girl was contending with serious issues of survival and safety at an age when most middle-class white girls were being protected and carefully prepared for a successful marriage" (61). Early novels about white girls suggest happiness is within the girl's power. These novels replicate a system of thought that says the clean body represents the moral integrity of the girl rather than the economic privilege of access to soap and water. The clean (white) girl "deserves" to be safe in this model; the worn clothing and bodies of girls with less racial or social privilege simultaneously marks them as less deserving of protection. The early girls' book teaches girls to do gender in an intersectional context. Because it defines a particular kind of household and set of family rituals as desirable—and suggests that following the rules of (northern) white families is what protects girls from assault, harassment, and deprivation—the girls' book contributes to the process of what Debby Irving calls "learning to be white."

The Development of the Girls' Book

Traditionally, Anglo-American literary scholars have described classic literature for girls as belonging to one of three categories: the moral tale, the family story, or the orphan girl novel. The earliest of these genres, the moral tale, is exemplified by Sarah Fielding's 1749 novel, *The Governess*. Fielding's novel tells the story of Jenny Peace and her schoolmates, who advance their moral education by hearing, telling, and discussing both autobiographical stories and fairy tales. Girl characters in *The Governess* are taught to interpret stories; they learn how to find the moral in a text and apply it to their own lives. Novels that similarly focused on educating rather than entertaining girls remained prominent through the first half of the nineteenth century. In such works, the act of telling a story presumed the girl's ignorance and need for explicit instruction on how to live a good life. Other early examples include Joachim Heinrich Campe's *Väterlicher Rath für meine Tochter* (Fatherly Advice for My Daughter) (1789) and Maria Edgeworth's *Moral Tales* (1801).

In the second half of the nineteenth century, with texts such as Alcott's *Little Women*, the focus shifted to engrossing tales of family life, in which character development and the reader's intimate engagement in a fictional world dominate. Moral instruction remained part of the genre, but now it was provided by a loving mother in the course of daily life, rather than by an abstract narrator or authoritarian adult. Here, the genre of girls' fiction overlaps with the family story, which Brian Attebery defines as "an essentially comic work with a collective hero" (115). While many readers see Jo March as the most engaging of the characters in *Little Women*, her journey unfolds within a family circle that provides safety but also constricts. *Little Women* relies on multiple protagonists for its narrative and reaches closure with an image of a mother surrounded by her daughters.

A third category of girls' fiction is the orphan girl novel, which differs from the family story in emphasizing the girl's vulnerability. The orphan girl novel takes as its primary influence the sentimental novel for women. Beginning in the eighteenth century, sentimental fiction became tremendously popular and included texts ranging from Samuel Richardson's novels to Susan Warner's *The Wide, Wide World* (1850).[6] The sentimental novel recounted the lives of women and the dramas of domesticity, focusing on amplifying the reader's emotional experience. Other relevant influences include texts such as Harriet Wilson's *Our Nig* (1859) and Harriet Jacobs's *Incidents in the Life of a Slave Girl* (1861)—books aimed at adult readers that describe both the exploitation and power of girls of color. *Our Nig* tells the story of a free Black girl whose suffering exposes the violence of racist structures in both the American North and South as well as the orphan girl's resilience. Similarly, in the orphan girl novel, a series of disasters leaves a girl alone in a hostile world, forced to make her own way and create a new family for herself.

Martha Finley's 1867 *Elsie Dinsmore* is perhaps the first of the orphan girl novels written for girls. Though Elsie does have a father, his neglect and the abuse she suffers at the hands of adults mark her story as linked to earlier domestic fiction in which an unhappy home life motivates the protagonist to develop inner resources and to construct a new family for herself. In the later Canadian novel *Anne of Green Gables* (1908), Anne finds herself at the mercy of a world in which she is valued for the labor she provides rather than loved because she is someone's daughter or sister. It becomes Anne's responsibility to shape her community into a loving family and she does so through her innate gifts of spirit and innocence. The novel for girls relies on heroines who are less perfect than Samuel Richardson's Clarissa, whose lack of autonomy emphasizes her lack of responsibility and also her inability to shape her life. In contrast, the protagonists of girls' books are responsible for their mistakes and capable of making choices that will influence the future course of their lives.

Both the family story and the orphan girl novel are examples of realistic fiction and linked to the Bildungsroman. The classic example of that genre, Goethe's *Wilhelm Meisters Lehrjahre* (1796), tells the realistic, if implausible, story of a young man who is motivated by his lover's betrayal to set off on a journey to make his way in the world. Less explicitly didactic than earlier moral tales, and focused on domestic coincidence rather than supernatural intervention, this Bildungsroman created a model of an extended discussion of an individual's social and psychological development as an apt subject for fiction. Later novels, such as Charlotte Brontë's *Jane Eyre* (1847), expanded the journey of personal development to female protagonists.

While girls' books are more likely to be linked to domestic realism than to the supernatural, they also often include elements of the uncanny and draw from texts as diverse as the Gothic romance *The Mysteries of Udolpho* (1794) and *Grimms' Fairy Tales* (1812). By appealing to magic and fantasy to explain the mysteries lying beneath the surface of daily life, they explore psychological complexity through metaphor. When Mary hears a mysterious cry in *The Secret Garden*, for example, she is participating in a long tradition of heroines who must rely on their own resources to decipher the truth of their situation.

Texts in all three categories are marked as girls' fiction in various ways. They are addressed to the girl reader, and they feature a girl protagonist (or protagonists), a circumscribed perspective (we see what the girl protagonist sees), and a shortened timeframe (the story usually takes place over a year or two).[7] For example, best-selling author Elizabeth Prentiss wrote both for women and for girls; her novel *Stepping Heavenward* (1869) is the journal of Katherine Mortimer from age sixteen through suffering adulthood as a wife and mother. In contrast, Prentiss's novel for girls, *The Flower of the Family: A Book for Girls* (1853), focuses on Lucy's year and a half away from home with summary reference to her later life. The girls' book also features simpler language and shorter sentences than fiction intended for adults, though the complexity of its plot and character development marks it as being for girls who are already proficient readers.

And while "classic" girls' books imagine a white readership, in fact, sanctioned literacy was only part of the story. As critics such as Katharine Capshaw and Anna Mae Duane, Jacqueline Jones Royster, Nazera Sadiq Wright, and Vanessa Steinroetter help us see, people of color in nineteenth-century America found ways to gain access to literacy even when formal systems did not support their education. Middle-class Black families encouraged their daughters' reading, stories written for Black girls appeared in magazines aimed at a Black readership, and the figure of the Black girl was imagined as a powerful force for the development of the Black family.[8]

In its earliest examples, however, the girls' book assumes whiteness as an identity and an ideal. Later examples of the genre also include protagonists from a variety of ethnic and racial backgrounds, living in varied family settings. As I discuss in the conclusion, understanding the early girls' book also has implications for our readings of more recent texts with nonwhite protagonists such as Virginia Hamilton's *Sweet Whispers, Brother Rush* (1982), Guadalupe Garcia McCall's *Under the Mesquite* (2011), and Nalo Hopkinson's *The Chaos* (2012).

A Distinct Subgenre

What is missing in the above history of girls' fiction is a group of best-selling books that originate in the mid-nineteenth century before both the family story and the orphan girl novel and that foreground adolescence as a category of identity. These stories assume the protected world of the family story but describe heroines who leave home to reimagine their identities. Anglo-American critics, from Nina Baym to Gillian Avery to Joe Sutliff Sanders, tell a story about the evolution of the American novel for girls that focuses on the orphaned girl protagonist who is subject to abuse by a spinster aunt and who uses her innocence to transform those who mistreat her.[9] But in fact, many of the earliest novels addressed to girl readers begin with an adolescent heroine rather than concluding with the heroine's adolescence. They describe a white protagonist who enjoys a loving family and whose journey is to a kind and wise female mentor, and they rely on a girl whose task is to transform herself rather than her community.

Here a British text for adult readers provides a useful model for the early adolescent girls' book. Jane Austen's *Northanger Abbey* (1817) describes the journey of young Catherine Morland, who leaves her happy home and family for the opportunity to see the wider world. While the satirical narrator of *Northanger Abbey* certainly presumes an adult audience, the plot structure helps us see how the dangers of the gothic novel can be reframed in a domestic model, and how it is possible for a girl to have social adventures without being left alone in the world. While Catherine is in danger at times, and lacks a good education that might protect her from uncomfortable moments, the narrator's control of the narrative and obvious affection for Catherine prevent us from feeling too much concern about Catherine's eventual success. She is a silly girl, but unlike the gothic heroines about whom she loves to read, her world is a more circumscribed and protected one. She lives in civilized England, not an imagined gothic Italy. Catherine's story models three key elements that will become central to the early adolescent girls' novel: the foundation of a loving, intact family; the journey away from home that makes her feel awkward and in need of education; and the engagement that marks the end of her story. While in Britain stories like Catherine's remained directed at adult readers, this plot appeared in the second half of the nineteenth century in both Germany and the United States in novels for girls. In Germany, books that describe the adolescent heroine's journey from home are called *Backfischliteratur*, and it is the Backfisch and her story that are the focus of the following chapters.

While the heroines of the Backfisch novel may weep like a sentimental heroine, the books themselves are not particularly religious or sentimental. Backfisch stories are not sensation novels, focused on the supernatural; the protagonists live realistic domestic lives without mysterious coincidences or dark passages. They are not family stories; the protagonists leave home and their families. They are framed more narrowly than the Bildungsroman; they emphasize the hard work of adolescence, not the organic growth of an individual over a lifetime.[10]

In an Anglo-American context, girls' books have typically been read through the lens of family—its presence or absence; if instead we consider girls' books through a German-American lens, the adolescent girl, as an individual who can best be educated outside of the family circle, comes into focus. When we examine the mid-nineteenth-century American best-seller lists with the German model of the Backfisch story in mind, a new set of texts emerges in the American history of girls' fiction. Germany and America are in fact linked in the production of novels for the adolescent girl, novels that focus not on the girl's ability to transform her community, but on her ability to transform herself into a young woman. Backfisch books lay out a space in between the protection (and confinement) of the family story and the vulnerability of the later orphan girl novel. They reveal another strand in the development of the girls' book, one in which girls are loved, protected, and expected to function independently of parents and siblings.

The Backfisch Book

Thienemann Press's series "Freche Mädchen, Freche Bücher" (Sassy Girls, Sassy Books) dominates the girls' section of German bookstores. While these bright paperbacks emphasize their hip, contemporary perspective on girls' lives, they are also linked to the nineteenth-century Backfisch book. For example, Hortense Ullrich's popular novel *Hexen Küsst man nicht* (*Witches Don't Get Kissed*) (1999) begins with the narrator's ironic comment that a diary—her most recent present from her aunt—is exactly what she wanted. While Josephine sees a diary as only marginally better than the pajamas that are her standard birthday present from her aunt, the inscription in the diary hints at the fact that this diary will exceed her expectations. Her aunt writes: "Dear Josephine! My diary was for me the most important companion through my Backfisch period" (3). By invoking the language of a "Backfisch period" and linking the written word to personal development, the author connects Josephine's own experience of adolescence to the lives of generations of women who came before her and the shared experience of reading.

Until I spent a semester at the Goethe University in Frankfurt, Germany, I had never heard the word *Backfisch*. But suddenly, as I began to read German girls' books, the word was everywhere. And while the Backfisch was most prominent in the nineteenth-century German novels I was reading, the word also appeared in texts as diverse as Johann Goethe's 1773 play *Götz von Berlichingen*, Charlotte Yonge's 1888 novel *Beechcroft at Rockstone*, and the German version of Cary Grant's 1947 film *The Bachelor and the Bobby-Soxer*.[11] The word was first used in the sixteenth century as a colloquial term to describe immature university students. It draws on both the Latin *baccalaureus* (young student) and the fishing term *Backfisch*, which describes fish not obviously large enough to take to market nor small enough to return to the water or use as bait. These middle-sized fish are thrown to the "back" of the boat to await the results of the day's catch. In the event the catch is poor and the *Backfisch* are taken to market, they will best be baked or fried to preserve their "jugendlichen Zartheit" (young tenderness) (Kluge, *Etymologisches Wörterbuch*). In the mid-nineteenth century, German authors used this word to highlight the category of female adolescence. It emphasizes the liminal status of a girl in her teens who is herself uncertain about her identity and appears to lack power over her social conditions.

As a term for an awkward adolescent girl, definitions of the "Backfisch" appear occasionally in English. The *Oxford English Dictionary* cites the 1891 *Pall Mall Gazette*: "Let us introduce the word 'Backfisch,' for we have the Backfisch always with us. She ranges from 15 to 18 years of age, keeps a diary, climbs trees secretly, blushes on the smallest provocation, and has no conversation." Mrs. Alfred Sidgwick, in her 1908 book *Home Life in Germany*, claims, "It is a girl who has left school but has not cast off her school-girl manners; and who, according to her nation and her history, will require more or less last touches" (36). In E. M. Forster's 1910 novel *Howard's End*, a note tells us Backfisch is "derogatory slang for a young woman"; the derogatory sense of the word was probably tied to its sexual connotations. G. Stanley Hall, the man credited with introducing the concept of adolescence into English-speaking culture, also uses the word. He writes in 1909, "'Backfisch' is a colloquial German term for a girl in the very earliest teens, and I use it here because I know of none in English or any other language so expressive, and because the age is as unique as the name" ("The Budding Girl").

The fish's period of indeterminacy parallels the teenage girl's uncertainty about her links to both childhood and adulthood. From the perspective of her social role, the Backfisch has no value because she can't yet be married. The Backfisch was ignored not simply because of her size, but because she was not yet "mannbar"—a word that translates directly as "marriageable" but literally means "man-full." Nevertheless, creating a literature for the Backfisch herself both establishes and explores the significance of adolescent girlhood and reimagines the negative connotations of the word. If the Backfisch is seen only in terms of her desirability to men, she is awkward and unformed—not yet ready for market. Significantly, the Backfisch book focuses not on the girl's eventual marriage but on the liminal space of her development, and it names that space as protected and creative. The Backfisch thus becomes a symbol of the possibilities of female adolescence. In a fictional world that honors her lack of stable identity and provides support for her education and growth, the Backfisch can learn to value her own transformative potential.

During the "Golden Age" of German girls' literature, which Gisela Wilkending describes as extending from the middle of the nineteenth century to the First World War, over two hundred German-speaking female authors published novels, narratives, and advice books for "little" and "young" girls ("Einleitung" 35). Backfisch books provide one of the central threads of this literature, which developed out of the German moral tales, the *Wandlungsgeschichte* or *Umkehrgeschichte* (transformation tale; story of conversion), and domestic fiction. These stories were intended for middle- or upper-class girls between the ages of fourteen and twenty who were between the worlds of school and marriage. The psychological qualities of puberty—in particular, the loss of a stable, childlike identity—made the Backfisch's story an interesting subject for novelists and led to the development of the genre of *Backfischliteratur* ("Einleitung" 52).

The Backfisch has typically experienced a free, unfettered childhood and experiences regret for its passing—much like the speaker of William Wordsworth's "Ode: Intimations of Immortality from Recollections of Early Childhood," who loses a childlike, unquestioning connection to nature. Wordsworth's poem reframes loss in terms of the "recompense" of art that growth allows. Similarly, the Backfisch discovers that maturity carries with it recompense for the loss of childhood; her story concludes not with longing for a more innocent past but with the optimistic anticipation of a future life. The Backfisch story—which focuses on the space between childhood and an independent mature identity—explores and honors what it means to be in transition.

Key to the plot is the heroine's need for improvement; she has bad manners, either through ignorance or willfulness, and needs the help of an older woman to improve herself. Like Anne of Green Gables, who "never makes the same mistake twice," many Backfisch heroines must work through a laundry list of bad behaviors. Backfisch heroines are loving, spontaneous, energetic, and—once motivated to change—capable of reforming themselves quickly. The issue for these girls is behavioral rather than moral—they are already good girls, and just need to learn to act in ways that allow others to see their virtues. Education is a source of power for these protagonists.

Indeed, these novels rely on the premise that education can shape their identity in ways that will lead to lasting happiness.

The Backfisch story focuses not on the girl's future (marriage and family), but on her present sense of purpose and power. Her story of escaping the comfort of home life by journeying to school or to relatives, often leaving the country for the city, provides an imaginative escape for readers, pushing them toward personal agency. Although the Backfisch novel often ends with engagement or marriage, the protagonist doesn't think about men at all until the last chapter(s); she is childlike and asexual.

The protagonist's sympathetic portrayal distinguishes Backfisch stories from earlier moral tales. The Backfisch book frames the protagonist's flaws as reflecting normal psychological development, rather than as a moral problem, as children's literature critic Dagmar Grenz points out (*Mädchenliteratur* 217). In the Backfisch book, the solution to the challenges of adolescence is to ensure girls are allowed a time of exploration and growth rather than forcing them too quickly into maturation. The Backfisch book redefines the protagonist's confusion about where she belongs as normal and productive. Engaging narration—usually in the form of a first-person narrative or a third-person narrative focalized through the heroine—creates an intimate experience for the reader and reinforces the protagonist's sympathetic portrayal.[12]

Although Backfisch books certainly participated in educating girls in patriarchal structures, nineteenth-century reviews suggest they also challenged social norms. As Wilkending explains, conservative critics saw the explosion of girls reading—especially reading love stories—as damaging established gender structures. Albrecht Goerth, the sharpest critic of Backfisch literature, argues that Backfisch narratives strengthened and provoked "die neue gefährliche Weiberkrankheit" (the new dangerous women's illness) and "Emanzipationssucht" (addiction to emancipation) (quoted in Wilkending, *Mädchenliteratur* 2). In identifying the act of reading girls' books as transgressive, critics acknowledged these books were doing more than socializing girls (Wilkending 2). In cultures where some saw the adolescent girl simply in terms of whether she was marriageable or not, these novels provided a different model, one that showed adolescence as a valuable time for self-transformation.[13]

Comparative Girls' Fiction

My project works to illuminate the genre of Backfisch literature by examining German and American texts comparatively to foster an understanding of nineteenth-century literature for and about girls well beyond the borders of either national literature. I take as foundational two claims by scholar Emer O'Sullivan in *Comparative Children's Literature*: 1) comparative study helps us identify the commonalities between different literatures as well as their "peculiarities and individual features"; and 2) interactions between literatures are essential to understanding their development (4). Much of the critical discussion of American girls' fiction has focused on the protagonist of the girls' story as a catalyst for transforming others; a comparative examination of Backfisch stories shows us a German-American genre focused on the adolescent girl who transforms herself rather than her community.

A close examination of the Backfisch novel as a German-American phenomenon reveals a poorly understood moment in children's literature when authors and readers alike explored girls' adolescence as a liminal time of exploration and growth. The term *Backfisch* and category of *Backfischliteratur* help us recognize patterns of storytelling that focused on the path from girlhood to womanhood in the nineteenth century and allow us to define a genre important to the history of the girls' book and the adolescent novel. The term can also help us see how nineteenth-century authors and readers in both Germany and the United States understood this liminal, dynamic, and often troubling phase of life, especially as that phase intersected with gendered norms. These novels reveal strategies for empowering girls that not only help us understand the nineteenth century and the girls' book better but also give us ideas for how to support contemporary adolescent girls.

Despite the extensive attention paid to early girls' books in both English- and German-language criticism, these texts have rarely been studied comparatively. The limited references to comparative study assume difference, suggesting that while early Anglo-American girls' books were family stories or orphan girl novels, German novels of the same period were stories of individual development.[14] There are several reasons for the absence of comparative work and lack of recognition of parallel examples of a genre of nineteenth-century adolescent fiction in the US and Germany. First, the fact that Britain and the United States share a language has led critics to focus on the Anglo-American girls' book, and nineteenth-century British girls' books tended to be family stories. Second, while the German language had a word to describe female adolescence in the mid-nineteenth century, English lacked a comparable term; thus this category of book was less visible in the history of US girls' fiction. Literary scholar Jaime Osterman Alves points out that "even as nineteenth-century Americans clearly struggled to define and understand adolescence, they did not yet have at their disposal a common language about, or uniform perception of, this distinct developmental stage" (5). Roberta Seelinger Trites notes the words "youth," "children," or "young people" would have varyingly been used to describe adolescence in nineteenth-century America (*Twain, Alcott* x). Phrases like "budding girl" (Hall) and "the awkward age" (Sarah Bilston) have not remained culturally significant. Recently, Katherine Magyarody reaches to the intriguing term "hobbledehoy" to explore nineteenth-century narratives of female development. Without a stable term to describe adolescence, Anglo-American critics have often missed the early emergence of the concept in girls' books.[15]

A lack of awareness of the connections between German and American girls' books may have more to do with the twentieth century than the nineteenth. Anti-German sentiment during World War I transformed American attitudes toward Germany. As a recent National Public Radio program put it, "During World War I, U.S. Government Propaganda Erased German Culture" (April 7, 2017). This erasure means the strong nineteenth-century ties between the two countries are remembered peripherally in the United States rather than being central to the cultural identity of both countries.

Bonds between Germany and the US were formed in three ways: through extensive German immigration to the US, through the travels of Americans to Germany, and through literary exchange and mutual appreciation. German immigrants hoping for greater access to education and property traveled to the United States, where they set up German printing presses and formed strong German-language communities. Almost a million Germans went to the United States during the 1850s, leading to a significant German-language presence in the US. Howell Heaney points out that "into the mid-19th century the laws and reports of Pennsylvania were printed in German as well as in English" (22). In Minnesota, a 1915 survey found that one hundred public one-room schoolhouses provided instruction mostly in German; more than two thirds of private schools in Minnesota at that time relied on German as the primary language of instruction (Rippley 176). Although before World War I 25 percent of American high school students studied German, by the end of the war, only 1 percent of high schools offered German (NPR).

But in the nineteenth century, American admiration for German language and culture was at its height. Travel in Germany was a standard practice for those with the means to augment a school education with study abroad. Alcott describes this practice in *Little Women* with both Laurie's and Amy's travels to the continent (and reminds us of German immigration with the character of Professor Bhaer and the Hummel family).[16] Alcott visited Europe twice and recorded her experiences of Germany in her journals; novelist Elizabeth Prentiss studied German, wrote letters about her admiration for Schiller and Goethe, and translated several hymns from the German; psychologist G. Stanley Hall's own interest in and awareness of female adolescence may have come from his time in Germany, where he studied philosophy. It is worth noting when Aunt Abigail provides comfort to Betsy in Canfield's *Understood Betsy*, she herself is immersed in Emerson's essays and the German-influenced transcendentalism he represented.

Most significantly, educated Germans and Americans felt a mutual respect and intellectual interest in the literary developments in both countries. Unitarian theologian Theodore Parker wrote in 1841 that "to our apprehension German literature is the fairest, the richest, the most original, fresh, and religious literature of all modern times" (Zacharasiewicz 26). And in an 1856 review in *American Publishers' Circular*, an editor wrote that "of all the living languages of Europe, there is not one more rich, original, idiomatic, and poetical, than the German. That language contains the finest and most useful, as well as beautiful specimens of modern Literature. To be ignorant of German—is not to know more than one-half of the Intellectual Culture of the last and present centuries" ("Review of the Week" 374).

The translation of German literature into English reflected close cultural bonds between the two countries, as Lynne Tatlock's compelling work demonstrates. For example, an 1869 review in the *Christian Examiner* claimed that "no bookstore is so small or so remote that German books do not make part of its stock, and help in its profits." The 1870 *Outline of German Literature* concluded that "the literature of the American nation" has "during recent years . . . more and more united itself with that of the German people" (Tatlock, "Domesticated Romance and Capitalist Enterprise" 155). Finally, an 1873 editorial in *Lippincott's Magazine* suggested the contributions of German women novelists "whose delineations have gained a popularity in America only less than that which they enjoy at home" are due "in part because the life which they depict has closer internal analogies to our own than to that of England or of France" (Tatlock, "German Women Writers and the North American Market" 38–39). The Prussian triumph in the Franco-Prussian war (1870–1871) added a sense of rising power to the aesthetic virtues of German culture (Zacharasiewicz 29).

In Germany, interest in American literature increased rapidly in the second half of the nineteenth century as American literature began to be recognized as distinct from British literature and of aesthetic value. Susan Warner's *The Wide, Wide World* was translated and well received as *Die Weite, Weite Welt* in 1853;[17] Harriet Beecher Stowe's *Uncle Tom's Cabin* was published in seventy-five editions in Germany (Vollmer 116). In 1868, K. Brunnermann published *Geschichte der Nordamerikanischen Literatur* (*A History of North American Literature*), an indication that American literature was beginning to be seen as a legitimate field of study as well as a means for practicing the English language.

Many of the best-selling Backfisch novels—in Germany and the United States—were translated and published in both countries. This is unsurprising, given that translation reached a peak in both countries in the 1880s (Tatlock, "Domesticated Romance and Capitalist Enterprise" 155). In "The American Novel in Germany, 1871–1913," Clement Vollmer points to an increased number of translations and interest in the American novel between 1882 and 1886, in part because inexpensive editions became available. Vollmer writes: "The Germans realized that the way to learn a language was to read copiously in that language, and to read something that interests as well as instructs. This trend of thought led naturally to the reading of the best that English and American literature offers, and was thus responsible largely for the keen interest in our novel" (128).

The urge to translate was no doubt encouraged by a lack of international copyright law. In European countries, policies attempting to provide protection for foreign authors—based on the idea that authors have natural rights to the product of their imaginations—began as early as the 1820s. The US, whose policies saw copyright as an economic issue designed to protect its nationals, didn't pass a law granting copyright protection to foreign authors until 1891.[18] The lack of copyright protection between the US and Germany meant best-selling novels in both countries were freely translated and republished.[19] All of the novels I discuss here were translated from their original language to English or German, most within a few years of their original publication. What resulted was a cross-cultural conversation about adolescent girlhood.[20]

While the immigration of Germans to the United States is a poorly remembered moment in American history, one of the impacts of this migration shows up in the nineteenth-century girls' book. In the twenty-first century, the story of influence is transmitted through fast electronic communication; in the nineteenth century, children's literature was shaped by a slower, but significant, cross-cultural interchange between Germany and the US. Comparative study reminds us cultures don't exist in isolation and the movement of bodies and books has a lasting influence on the history of ideas.

Imagining Adolescence

Contemporary discussions of adolescence begin with the premise that we know what adolescence is—disorderly, alienated, a problem. Hidden behind these descriptors is the idea that adolescence must be this way and that its definition lies not just in a stage of life, the period between childhood and adulthood, but also in its painful difference from either category. While critics disagree about when adolescence enters American culture as a concept, they concur it is a transitional state, what Hall calls "the most plastic stage of temperament and character" (*Adolescence* 364). Later critics reaffirm this sense of adolescence as a "process of becoming" (Baxter 11), a "provisional free space" (Mitchell 9), an "indefinable space between innocence and experience, or asexuality and sexuality" (Waller 30).

In her foundational book *American Childhood*, Anne Scott MacLeod provides multiple examples of the ways nineteenth-century writers saw the movement from childhood to adulthood as the "decisive moment in a girl's life" and "a dramatic event" (14). Lynne Vallone focuses on images of adolescent girlhood as a "dangerous time" in eighteenth- and nineteenth-century books for girls and adults. Later discussions of the classic girls' book tend not to acknowledge adolescence. It is seen as a category that doesn't appear in popular culture until the end of the nineteenth century and doesn't appear in children's literature until the mid-twentieth century. More recent studies, including books by Sally Mitchell and Beth Rodgers, propose that British books and magazines acknowledge an adolescent female reader as early as the 1880s. As the books I discuss in this project demonstrate, mid-nineteenth-century German and American novels for girls focus on adolescent heroines and acknowledge adolescence as a transitional phase of life, separate from childhood and womanhood.

Adolescence is both a biological process, shaped by the advent of puberty, and a socially constructed and varied concept. It relies on material changes in both the body and the culture. In societies such as nineteenth-century America and Germany, the gap between the age of menarche and the age of marriage allowed a space for adult fears about unsanctioned female sexuality and the problem of what to do with girls who were biologically mature and yet culturally considered too young for marriage. One solution was the creation of a literature that might entertain without overtaxing the vulnerable brains of adolescent girls. Here we see social changes—such as increased literacy rates and disposable income—unite with cultural anxiety and biology.[21]

For decades, the dominant voice in American discussions of adolescence was that of Hall, who is often seen as "inventing" adolescence with his 1904 book *Adolescence: Its Psychology and its Relations to Physiology, Anthropology, Sociology, Sex, Crime, Religion and Education*. Certainly Hall's work was pivotal in popularizing adolescence; his focus on the "storm and stress" of adolescence and its link to juvenile delinquency helped shape the image of the alienated teenager that continues to hold power in contemporary discourse. Hall's work builds on that of Jean-Jacques Rousseau, who wrote in 1762 that puberty is linked to "a change of temper, frequent outbreaks of anger, a perpetual stirring of the mind" and that the adolescent "becomes deaf to the voice he used to obey; he is a lion in fever; he distrusts his keeper and refuses to be controlled" (*Émile* Book IV). In his useful discussion of the ways adolescence served as a "scapegoat" for "fears and anxieties" that permeated American culture at the turn of the twentieth century, literary historian Kent Baxter argues the concept of the estranged adolescent emerged because it embodied "all that was threatening about 'modern life'" (3).

Hall's reliance on Rousseau's model of the male adolescent—a "savage" who must resist adult authority in order to become an independent citizen—led to studies of adolescence that took the white, male, middle-class body as the norm. More recently, some critics have asked how definitions of adolescence change when we consider girlhood. Two important works—Crista DeLuzio's *Female Adolescence in American Scientific Thought, 1830–1930* and Rodgers's *Adolescent Girlhood and Literary Culture at the Fin de Siecle: Daughters of Today*—expand the study of adolescence in the nineteenth century to girls. DeLuzio helps us see the ways the work of contemporary psychologists such as Carol Gilligan have roots in nineteenth-century studies of adolescent girlhood; Rodgers draws on diverse examples of girlhood in literary texts to propose adolescent girlhood "attained a new kind of significant symbolic value in the closing decades of the nineteenth century" (2).

By expanding the study of adolescence to girls, these critics make two important points. First, adolescence appeared as a significant category in American culture before Hall popularized the concept. Second, Hall's focus on "storm and stress" as fundamental to adolescence is not a universal model; earlier discussions of female adolescence suggest adolescence can be a welcome period of transformation. If we assume adolescence is characterized by alienation and independence, it appears to be a category incompatible with the successful performance of femininity. By looking at descriptions of adolescent girlhood in literary texts, an alternate and more positive model of adolescence emerges. In *Juvenile Literature and British Society, 1850–1950*, Charles Ferrall and Anna Jackson claim some early books for girls represent adolescence as "a time of principled idealism, action, and aspiration" (70); Rodgers agrees many nineteenth-century texts focus on the "positive nature of the changes taking place in girls' lives . . . heroism, creativity, community, resourcefulness" (11); Allison Giffen and Robin L. Cadwallader suggest that "girlhood is a dynamic site that extends the thrilling promise for agency and social action" (6–7). These texts clarify that fiction, not just psychology or sociology, both represents and produces ideas of adolescence (Waller 1).

The genre of Backfisch literature adds to these discussions by providing a word and definition to identify the nineteenth-century adolescent girl, emphasizing the role of German culture in American conceptions of adolescence and extending her history to the mid-nineteenth century. In his 2007 book, *Teenage: The Creation of Youth Culture,* Jon Savage describes two mid-century adolescents as "harbingers of a new intermediate state that as yet had no name" (13). While there is no word for "adolescent boy" in nineteenth-century Germany, the word *Backfisch* appears as early as 1555 as a word for a "half-grown girl" (Kluge 43). The definition of the term is most famously documented in the saying: "Vierzehn Jahre sieben Wochen ist der Backfisch ausgekrochen. Siebsehn Jahre Wochen drei ist die Backfischzeit vorbei" (At fourteen years and seven weeks emerges the Backfisch. At seventeen years and three, the Backfisch time is past.) In mid-century Germany, the white, middle-class girl had not only an identity, but also a literature of her own. Yet despite this clear model and Hall's exposure to it when he studied psychology in Germany in the late 1870s, when Hall conceptualizes adolescence, he takes Rousseau's model of the savage boy rather than a German model of the awkward girl as a starting point. Thus, the twentieth-century American teenager is established as a vessel for anxieties about wild teenagers on city streets rather than as a metaphor for transformation and growth.

If we start with an image of an adolescent girl as a loveable, awkward person in need of education and support in order to become a good woman and wife, adolescence is difficult for girls themselves, but not for the adults around them. These nineteenth-century girls are presented as needing empathy rather than scorn or fear. Even the later Backfisch, who may be a tomboy (for example, Ilse in *An Obstinate Maid* or Katy in *What Katy Did*), is exuberant rather than savage. Wilkending points to the fact that the "wild Backfisch" and her period of storm and stress were taken positively because the girl's rebellion was framed as an example of courage and strength and her situation defined as temporary (*Mädchenliteratur* 31). The Backfisch book illuminates an alternate model of adolescence, one that imagines the space between childhood and adulthood as creative, flexible, and beneficial to both the adolescent and her community. Late nineteenth-century fears about independent adolescents and a culture that increasingly left teenagers to make their own way to adulthood led to a split between what Baxter calls the "real" and the "ideal" adolescent—one delinquent, the other obedient. In the Backfisch book, we are offered a third option—the adolescent girl who struggles without rejecting adults, who is well mentored and values that mentoring. The conservative, gendered plot arc that tells girls happiness comes with obedience and marriage also allows for a vision of adolescence as delightful.

In later girls' books and narratives of adolescence, the sweetness of the Backfisch—her open sociability and exuberance—is transferred to the younger girl protagonist, so the adolescent can be redefined in terms of her opposition to the adult world and the angst this produces for both adolescents and adults. The Backfisch book suggests adolescent recalcitrance is a product of the adult imagination. In A. D. T. Whitney's *Faith Gartney's Girlhood*, for example, the secondary heroine, Glory, is an Irish-American orphan who is exploited by a cruel mistress. The woman defines Glory as conniving and lazy; as readers, we know she is loyal, committed, and creative.

In 1928, Margaret Mead asked in *Coming of Age in Samoa*: "If it is proved that adolescence is not necessarily a specially difficult period in a girl's life . . . then what accounts for the presence of storm and stress in American adolescence?" (qtd. in Baxter 63–64). The stress of adolescence in the Backfisch novel is the immaturity of adults who don't understand their own responsibility for nurturing teenaged girls. In the Backfisch book, healthy adults have their own friends and projects, see themselves as allies, believe they can be helpful, and are successful at shaping girls into good women. In part, this is because they are not confused about what a good woman looks like—there is a clear, gendered template and they trust in the education they provide. By 1885, the narrative had begun to shift. In *Der Troztkopf* (*An Obstinate Maid*), Ilse is sent away to school because her parents don't know how to shape her into a woman. The headmistress at the school is also at a loss and throws up her hands at Ilse's obstinacy. These novels suggest a model of alienated adolescence originates in adult anxiety over the work of raising girls.

Literature aimed at adolescent girls on both sides of the Atlantic adds to the evidence that the shaping of women was a concern for authors and readers decades before the word "adolescent" entered popular discourse in America. In fact, the pattern of the Backfisch novel gives us valuable insight into how the qualities, risks, and needs of adolescence were defined as early as the 1850s. While this genre is in some ways socially conservative, it also provides us with vivid models for thinking about female adolescence as significant and transformative. Its patterns allow us to see how girls can be powerful actors and adults significant allies even within a sexist society. The term *Backfisch* reveals what has remained hidden in Anglo-American discussions of the girls' book: a concept of adolescent girlhood in nineteenth-century America, the existence of early adolescent literature that accommodates anxieties about female maturation, and the connections between American and German girls' fiction.

Examples of the Backfisch Genre

This project takes Clementine Helm's 1863 *Backfischen's Leiden und Freuden* (*Gretchen's Joys and Sorrows*) as an exemplar of the genre and moves both backward—to earlier American novels that follow a similar pattern—and forward—to German and American texts that develop the genre. It examines eight best-selling Backfisch novels written between 1853 and 1885, many of which remain in print today, all of which were published in both German and English. These novels expose the transatlantic connections that made the adolescent girl of particular interest to America and Germany in the second half of the nineteenth century. They provide a key addition to a genealogy of the novel for girls of all ages and reveal that the young adult novel began not in the mid-twentieth century but a hundred years earlier.

The novels I discuss—four originally written in German, four in English—represent the most successful of their genre in the marketplace (hence their translation and republication). Two are well known to contemporary English-speaking audiences (Alcott's *An Old-Fashioned Girl* and Johanna Spyri's *Heidi*). All, I argue, influenced the evolution of girls' fiction and provide insight into our understanding of nineteenth-century female adolescence. While cultural differences certainly exist between Germany and the United

Frontispiece. From *Backfischen's Leiden und Freuden: Eine Erzählung für junge Mädchen* (Leipzig: Georg Wigand's Verlag, 1880).

States, these novels present similar ideas about the work of becoming a woman.[22] Read comparatively, they make visible the patterns and concerns of this central early genre of girls' fiction.

I analyze four German-language novels by the following writers: Clementine Helm (1825–1926), Eugenie Marlitt (1825–1887), Emmy von Rhoden (1829–1885), and Johanna Spyri (1827–1901). All four women were tremendously successful as authors—von Rhoden only after her death—and all contributed to the development of the girls' book. These four German-speaking authors were born in the mid-1820s, at a time when their national identity would have been linked to individual states (or in Spyri's case, to Switzerland) rather than to a single nation-state.[23] They were united by their participation in a German literary tradition. While as a Swiss woman Spyri did not share a German national identity, the language boundaries within Switzerland meant there was little literary contact between that country's linguistic regions (Eigler and Kord 507). Thus, the German-speaking Spyri had a close connection to German authors who shared her language, and her novel *Heidi* was influential in its construction of an idealized, natural Switzerland for German readers.

The paradigmatic Backfisch novel—which German critics use to define the genre—is Helm's 1863 *Backfischen's Leiden und Freuden* (*Gretchen's Joys and Sorrows*, 1877; *A Miss in Her Teens*, 1877). *Gretchen's Joys and Sorrows* was the most successful of Helm's forty books; published in 1863, it was in its fiftieth edition by 1897. In this first-person narrative, sixteen-year-old Gretchen leaves her loving family in the country to be educated by her aunt in Berlin. Her identity as a Backfisch is linked to her awkwardness, her good heart, and her willingness to be educated. I place in relation to this novel six other "Backfisch novels" and a transitional novel, *Heidi*, that rely on a similar pattern to tell their stories. Together, these texts provide us with examples that develop the complexity and variation present in the genre.

Marlitt's 1871 *Das Heideprinzeßchen* (*The Little Moorland Princess*, 1872; *The Little Princess*, 1883; *The Princess of the Moor*, 1890) shows how the basic Backfisch plot—of a girl who needs an education to smooth her rough edges—can be intertwined with gothic and

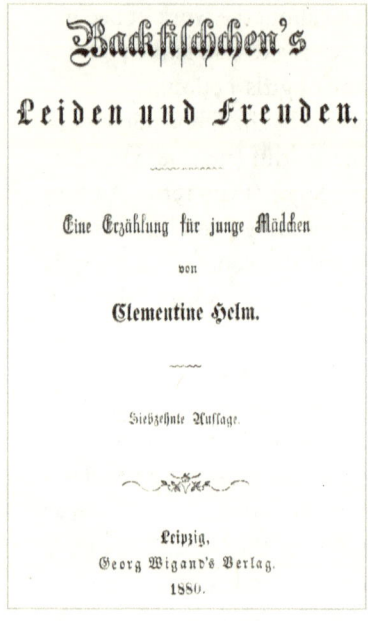

Title page. *Backfischen's Leiden und Freuden: Eine Erzählung für junge Mädchen* (Leipzig: Georg Wigand's Verlag, 1880).

Title page. *Gretchen's Joys and Sorrows* (Boston: A. Williams & Co., 1877).

sensational elements.[24] The protagonist Lenore shares with other Backfisch girls the ability to transform herself through hard work and deliberate application. Although originally aimed at adult readers, the novel was adapted by Marie Otto for girls and published in German in 1889 as *Heideprinzeßchen*. The popularity of this adaptation—which went through multiple editions—speaks to the ways *The Little Moorland Princess* relies on the structure of a Backfisch novel. The novel's English translations use a less complex language, suggesting a dual audience. *The Little Moorland Princess* remained culturally significant well into the twentieth century; a 1918 film version of the novel was directed by Georg Victor Mendel, and a new edition of the novel appeared as recently as 1994.

With von Rhoden's 1885 *Der Trotzkopf: Eine Pensionsgeschichte für Junge Mädchen* (*An Obstinate Maid*, 1898; *Taming a Tomboy*, 1898), the Backfisch novel became more closely aligned with the tomboy figure and school story. An immediate bestseller, the novel

Cover. *Der Trotzkopf* (68th edition. Stuttgart: Gustav Weise Verlag, n.d.).

Title page. *Der Trotzkopf* (68th edition. Stuttgart: Gustav Weise Verlag, n.d.).

Frontispiece. *An Obstinate Maid* (Philadelphia: George W. Jacobs, 1898).

Title page. *An Obstinate Maid* (Philadelphia: George W. Jacobs, 1898).

Cover. *Taming a Tomboy* (New York: A. L. Burt, 1898).

Title page. *Taming a Tomboy* (New York: A. L. Burt, 1898).

was in its sixty-eighth edition by the turn of the twentieth century; its popularity in the twentieth century was further bolstered by a 1983 television miniseries.

The four American authors I discuss—Elizabeth Prentiss (1818–1878), A. D. T. Whitney (1824–1906), Louisa May Alcott (1832–1888), and Susan Coolidge (1835–1905)[25]—were all prolific writers who wrote novels for readers of all ages. All four of these women spent most of their lives in New England and identified as northerners.

Elizabeth Prentiss wrote the earliest of the Backfisch books, which is also perhaps the first novel for girls in America: *The Flower of the Family: A Book for Girls* (1853).[26] Her works are the most explicitly Christian of the authors I include and continue to be popular on lists of Christian novels for girls and women. What distinguishes *The Flower of the Family* from earlier sentimental novels for women is a less complex diction that marks it as young

Cover. *The Flower of the Family* (New York: Anson D. F. Randolph, 1883).

Title page. *The Flower of the Family* (New York: Anson D. F. Randolph, 1883).

adult fiction, a focus on validating Lucy's own perspective on her life and troubles and the assurance that Lucy lives in a protected world, which allows her to focus on her own development rather than on her survival.

While all of the authors I discuss were popular in their own time, Louisa May Alcott's work has remained beloved by a wide audience of readers and critics to the present day. *An Old-Fashioned Girl* was the first of Alcott's novels to be translated into German and, according to the *German American Annals*, the only American novel to be published in Germany in German in 1872.[27] The English text of this novel was also published in Germany in 1883 as part of the Tauchnitz series. Unlike *Little Women*, with its focus on the growth of a family through stories of individual girls, *An Old-Fashioned Girl* replicates the pattern of the Backfisch novel by following a single

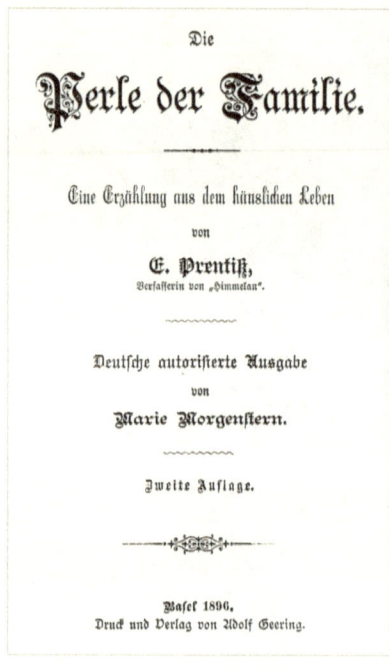

Cover. *Die Perle der Familie* (Basel: Adolf Geering, 1896).   Title page. *Die Perle der Familie* (Basel: Adolf Geering, 1896).

protagonist—Polly—as she learns to balance her playful girlishness with mature womanhood.

A. D. T. Whitney's books, like those by Prentiss, were often marketed as "Sunday-school books" that combined literary appeal with a moral education. Her novel *Faith Gartney's Girlhood* (1863) works with a double heroine to provide contrasting examples of how adolescent girls can find meaningful work in the world. Susan Coolidge's *What Katy Did: A Story* (1872) has much in common with *An Obstinate Maid*; it also takes an exuberant girl and considers the kind of shaping that will make that girl into a healthy woman. The novel was made into a television miniseries (1962) and two television movies (1972, 1999).

My discussion of the Backfisch novel concludes by bringing the Swiss *Heidi* into the conversation as a text that helps us see the

Ein Mädchen

aus der

Guten alten Schule

von

Louisa M. Alcott.

Für die reifere Jugend

aus dem Englischen übersetzt

von

Mary C. Rothwell.

Stuttgart.
Verlag von Wilhelm Nitzschke.

Title page. *Ein Mädchen aus der guten alten Schule* (Stuttgart: Verlag von Wilhelm Nitzschke, 1860).

THE HUT OF THE ALM-UNCLE

Frontispiece. *Heidi: A Little Swiss Girl's City and Mountain Life* (Boston: Ginn, 1899).

movement from girls' books focused on awkward adolescence to girls' books that idealize the girl child. Johanna Spyri first published *Heidi* in two parts in 1880 and 1881 as *Heidis Lehr- und Wanderjahre* (*Heidi. Her Years of Wandering and Learning*, 1884) and *Heidi Kann Brauchen, Was Es Gelernt Hat* (*How She Used What She Learned*, 1884). The novel's link to German literature is not only linguistic; it was first popular in Germany, parts of the novel are set in Frankfurt, the novel's publisher was German, and Spyri directly places her novel in the German Bildungsroman tradition.[28] *Heidi* has been translated into fifty languages, and over fifty million copies have been sold.[29]

The chapters that follow explore the interactions between German and American Backfisch novels. The first chapter defines the protagonist at the heart of the Backfisch book and considers the free space that allows her to journey toward a mature identity. The second chapter examines mothering as a communal enterprise, drawing on the Black feminist concept of "othermothering" to explore how the Backfisch encounters support outside of the home. The third chapter shows how the Backfisch novel's insistence that domestic and emotional labor are crucial to the girl's maturation

HEIDI

A LITTLE SWISS GIRL'S CITY AND MOUNTAIN LIFE

BY

FRAU JOHANNA SPYRI

TRANSLATED FROM THE THIRTEENTH GERMAN EDITION

BY

HELEN B. DOLE

WITH ILLUSTRATIONS

GINN & COMPANY
BOSTON · NEW YORK · CHICAGO · LONDON

Title page. *Heidi: A Little Swiss Girl's City and Mountain Life* (Boston: Ginn, 1899).

draws on a common trope from the sentimental novel. The fourth chapter explores resonances between the domestic model of the Backfisch's journey and the larger project of nation-building and teaching whiteness. The fifth chapter uses Backfisch literature to complicate an assumption by many literary critics that girls' fiction is necessarily nostalgic, arguing that this strand of girls' fiction is an important precursor to the twentieth-century young adult novel, with its emphasis on personal development. The conclusion considers the implications of adding an awareness of the Backfisch novel to our readings of contemporary girls' fiction.

The Backfisch, as an image of the female adolescent, challenges us to acknowledge the agency and complexity of the growing girl. It broadens our understanding of the structure and appeal of girls' fiction as a genre that relies not only on images of the vulnerable girl child in distress but also on the empowered adolescent girl whose agency develops in a supportive community. While these conservative narratives rely on strict gender binaries, reinforce white privilege, and are limited in the options they can imagine for girls, the appeal of these stories comes not from their restrictive impulse but from the fantasies of growth they provide. In the world of the Backfisch, several key themes emerge—the importance of free space for transformation, the role of community in individual development, the effort shaping a mature identity requires, the impact of that identity on cultural narratives, and the value of maturity. I demonstrate that the genre is more flexible than a focus on later child heroines suggests and worthy of further critical attention.

Most significantly, these novels start with the premise that a girl protagonist is a fitting subject for stories about growing up. Fraught questions of human identity are assumed by these authors to be most interesting in the context of female-centered narratives. By framing female adolescence as positive and the challenges of maturation as productive, we have another stance from which to support the girls in our lives. The buffer *Understood Betsy*'s Cousin Abigail provides between Betsy and her fear of the unknown is at the center of the Backfisch novel. And perhaps for this reason, the girls' book speaks to adult readers as well as adolescent girls. There are times in our lives when we may also want to enter into the flexible, complex space modeled by the Backfisch. In the safety of imagined worlds, where being uncertain is encouraged and change is desirable, we can try on possible identities and imagine ourselves transformed.

· CHAPTER ONE ·
Defining the Backfisch

It's such a solemn thing to be almost fourteen, Marilla. Miss Stacy took all us girls who are in our teens down to the brook last Wednesday, and talked to us about it. She said we couldn't be too careful what habits we formed and what ideals we acquired in our teens, because by the time we were twenty our characters would be developed and the foundation laid for our whole future life.
(ANNE OF GREEN GABLES, 1908, CHAPTER 30)

When Anne Shirley comes home from school one day to muse with Marilla, "It is such a solemn thing to be almost fourteen," she seems a long distance from the child with a tear-stained face who arrived at Green Gables three years earlier. She is now valued for more than the work she provides; she has succeeded in making a place for herself in a family and in a community. Even more significantly, for the purposes of this chapter, Anne has the luxury of paying attention to herself as one of the "girls who are in our teens."

A year after the publication of *Anne of Green Gables*, G. Stanley Hall published an essay in *Appleton's Magazine* entitled "The Budding Girl." He writes,

> "Backfisch" is a colloquial German term for a girl in the very earliest teens, and I use it here because I know of none in English or any other language so expressive.... She is no longer a little girl, but by no means yet a young woman, nor is she a cross between or a mixture of the two, but a something quite unique and apart.... That is one reason why she is now the most intricate and baffling problem perhaps that science has ever yet attracted.

While Hall, like Miss Stacy, sees adolescent girlhood as worth acknowledging, he also sees it as a "baffling problem." Hall's assertion in 1909 that female adolescence was both a mystery and a "problem" reflected the perspective of scientists and politicians who saw the dual identity of unstable adolescence and hysterical femininity as a dangerous combination.[1] As I discuss in the introduction, his model of adolescence became the dominant one of the twentieth and twenty-first centuries, and it shaped a paradigm of adolescence based on the expectation that teenaged girls are defined by their mysterious difference from adults and the conflict that difference constructs.

Many girls' books of the time took a different perspective, portraying female adolescence not as perplexing difference but as a natural period of identity development; indeed, they suggest that girls have a right to a protected space for growth. While *Anne of Green Gables* begins as an orphan girl novel, by the time Miss Stacy takes Anne down to the brook she has repositioned herself as a valued member of her community. In its insistence on the girl's own agency and ability to shape her life rationally and productively, *Anne of Green Gables* draws on earlier novels for adolescent girls as well as on stories of neglected children. These novels provide a space by the brook and between their covers that recognizes adolescence as perhaps the most important phase of a girl's life, and they model how to make good use of that space. While these early girls' novels are unlikely to be popular reading for contemporary girls, they do provide an alternate, less fraught vision of adolescent girlhood and encourage us to ask how the successful strategies offered to the nineteenth- and early twentieth-century girl can be adapted to support twenty-first-century teenagers.

When Hall described female adolescence in his 1909 essay, he didn't use the word *adolescent*, a word he introduced into public discourse in 1904 (*Adolescence*)—instead, curiously, he used the word *backfisch*. While Hall appeals to the German language to understand the category of female adolescence, I use this term as a point of entry into an important genre of girls' fiction—books for adolescent girls published between 1853 and 1885. Starting with Clementine Helm's 1863 novel *Backfischen's Leiden und Freuden* (*Gretchen's Joys and Sorrows*), the German adolescent girl had not only a word to describe her liminal state but also a literature to entertain and instruct her. American authors both recognized and wrote for their own adolescent girls as early as 1853, when Elizabeth Prentiss published *The Flower of the Family*, but the English language lacked a popular and consistent term for female adolescence until the beginning of the twentieth century. German texts name both the adolescent girl (the Backfisch) and her short but crucial period of development (the *Backfischzeit*, or adolescent time), calling our attention to a shared German-American generic structure in girls' fiction of the 1850s, '60s, '70s, and '80s.

A German-American lens allows us to focus on the early novel for adolescent girls, in which mid-nineteenth-century authors in both countries acknowledged and created a space where the adolescent girl could be profitably uncomfortable and awkward, where she could make and learn from mistakes. Using popular examples of the genre from both countries, this chapter shows that both German Backfisch novels and their American counterparts highlight the ability of individual girls to engage in identity formation through the protection of a *Backfischzeit*. I argue that the term *Backfisch* provides a context from which we can recover understudied early novels for girls, novels that portray adolescence not as a space marked by hormonal distress and social alienation, but as a period that is solemn and significant.[2]

Also called *Wandlungsgeschichte* (transformation stories) by German-language critics, these novels acknowledge the confusion of this period in a girl's life but redefine that confusion as a creative space. This liminal space is both physical—the girl moves to a new location, away from her childhood home—and psychological—she enters into a period of self-reflection, provoked both by her own sense that her life is shifting and by new expectations exerted by others. Away from the expectations of her family, which sees her as a child, she can refashion herself. The experience of coming into contact with new ways of being and new ideas opens up a wider variety of choices, allowing her the flexibility to shift her identity.

The Backfisch's story is located in the space between her father's house and her husband's. She leaves home not because she must, but because she or her parents desire a different kind of life for her from what her parents' home can provide. Unlike the nineteenth-century female Bildungsroman, which moves from the childhood home through a brief period of independence to maturity (which for nineteenth-century women meant marriage and the confines of a husband's home), these novels take as their focus an adolescent heroine. They are framed more narrowly than the Bildungsroman in that their focus is the hard work of adolescence, not the organic growth of an individual over a lifetime.[3] Backfisch novels often introduce the girl's loving family to make it clear that she is not an abandoned orphan. The girl goes on a carefully mentored journey that provides opportunities for growth and even transformation, and her successful completion of this journey is marked by the appearance of a suitor/husband.

This chapter examines four early novels for girls—two written in English and two in German—to explore the significance and value of adolescent identity formation in the Backfisch book. I use translations of two German Backfisch novels—Clementine Helm's 1863 *Backfischen's Leiden und Freuden* (translated by Helen M. Dunbar Slack in 1877 as *Gretchen's Joys and Sorrows*) and Eugenie Marlitt's 1871 *Das Heideprinzeßchen* (translated by Mrs. A. L. Wister in 1872 as *The Little Moorland Princess*)—to lay out the qualities and complexities of the genre. The chapter then moves to two American girls' novels of the same period—Elizabeth Prentiss's 1853 *The Flower of the Family* and Louisa May Alcott's 1869 *An Old-Fashioned Girl*—to show how the pattern of the Backfisch novel appeared and developed in mid-nineteenth-century America.

Helm's *Gretchen's Joys and Sorrows* is the paradigmatic Backfisch book. It describes Gretchen, a sixteen-year-old girl and "poor little backfisch," who leaves her loving family in the country to visit her aunt in the city of Berlin (8). First published in 1863, the novel has gone through thirty-five editions, with the most recent edition published in 1998. The novel was translated twice into English—the United States edition cited here and a British edition, *A Miss in Her Teens*, both initially published in 1877. Gretchen is a "simple country girl" who is "pretty" and "dark-eyed" (32, 36). Her biggest faults are carelessness and an "excessive desire to please" (33). While her aunt has no problem with her country clothes, she does want her to learn to keep her things neat, clean, and well mended. Gretchen is tall and seems not quite to have her limbs under control. Her awkwardness is both physical and psychological—she is unsure of how to play her role as young lady (versus child) and as city girl (versus country girl). She is also a "natural" child, a term that appears again and again in descriptions of the heroines of the earliest books for girls (46). Her naturalness emphasizes her innocence and lack of artifice but also causes her trouble, as when she forgets her handkerchief and is unprepared to deal with a runny nose.

As with most Backfisch heroines, Gretchen's experience of the liminal space of adolescence is reflected in the literal transition of her journey from country to city, comfortable home to exciting society. Home was a place of simplicity, lack of correction, and familiarity. In Berlin, the spaces and people are foreign, and she is expected to follow different rules. The consequences for ignoring these rules are embarrassment, ridicule, unwanted attention, and shame; her excessive desire to please means she is horrified at every error. While her mortification aids her education, it is also a characteristic she needs to overcome. Gretchen needs to learn to move more cautiously through society and to be aware that her impulsive actions may be interpreted differently from what she intends. For example, after Gretchen receives an undesired proposal of marriage, her aunt scolds her, explaining that "many girls have fallen into coquetry simply because they were led by their thoughtlessness to say and do things which offend against the established rules of society" (38). Gretchen's aunt sees her flirtation as unconscious error rather than as reflecting her developing sexuality. This attitude is typical of the Backfisch story, which defines the girl's sexuality as something perceived by others.

Gretchen's education and the novel as a whole focus on the importance of making good choices and becoming a responsible woman. Gretchen learns partly by negative example; her uncle made a poor choice of second wife, who is a misery to him and a barrier to his daughter's proper education. Gretchen tells us, "His experience showed me what an important thing a proper education is, which nips in the bud all wrong and pernicious influences" (93). But unlike in earlier stories that frighten girls into good behavior, Gretchen and the reader also learn through her successes. Gretchen reflects, "I understood better and better how well for my intellectual development it was for me to spend a part of my youth with Aunt Ulrike, and the inexpressible love which she showed me, carried me more lightly through the thousand faults and mistakes against which I, poor backfischchen, had daily to struggle" (39). Moving to the city helps make Gretchen aware of her need for change. One of the essential qualities of the Backfisch story is that it acknowledges and values a *Backfischzeit* as both challenging, "die schwierige Backfischzeit" ("the difficult Backfisch time"), and rewarding. By leaving home and her everyday life, Gretchen can benefit from a protected period of education.

Gretchen's new world is full of rules, and the key is for her to learn to balance her natural, artless character with education, which will teach her how to act with appropriate restraint. Her friend Marie tells her, "We must quite too often place our feelings under restraint when we are among others, and still keep a quiet face, while in our hearts we may be as sad or joyful as we will" (16). The goal is to guard one's natural, emotional, loving heart behind a public persona of manners and restraint. Like Mrs. March from Alcott's *Little Women*, who hides her anger so well that Jo is surprised to learn she feels it, Gretchen must learn to keep her anger and her joy to herself. Her childlike effusiveness is lovely, but unchecked, it will subject her to the disdain of better-educated people, suggest that she is in love when she is merely being polite, and leave her open to excessive familiarity from people (especially men) she does not know. Ultimately, Gretchen must be both loving and self-restrained, a child of nature and a woman of society. Once mastered, these combinations will make her both sexually attractive and suitable as a wife. Without her artless charm, no man would be attracted to her; without self-control (and clean gloves), no man would want to marry her.

The tension here is between attracting the right man and avoiding the wrong ones, and the text repeatedly stresses this lesson. Men make rude comments to her, follow her through the streets, and even chase her through the woods. According to the narrative, it is the responsibility of those around her to protect Gretchen by teaching her the rules that apply to ladies: she must shape her appearance to match her virtue so that she can take advantage of the protections offered "good" girls. The plot of this novel, like the plots of most Backfisch novels, ends with Gretchen's marriage as a marker of her successful transformation into a young woman. Gretchen's happiness depends not on changing her community or her future partner but in using her *Backfischzeit* to learn how to take her proper role in a larger world.

My second example is Marlitt's *The Little Moorland Princess*, which was quickly translated into multiple English editions to huge acclaim. The novel focuses on the story of Lenore von Sassen, only daughter of a renowned scholar, and on her transformation from wild moorland child of seventeen to a loving, domestic bride who is not much older. Like *Gretchen's Joys and Sorrows*, the novel is written in the first person from a point in the future and hints at an educational purpose. These texts are conduct books as well as entertaining stories, and the first-person narrative allows the reader to enter into the heroine's emotional experience intimately.

We meet Lenore on her seventeenth birthday in the midst of a wild moorland scene, where we are introduced first to her "two small brown feet" standing in a stream and then to "two sunburnt hands" (4–5). Lenore describes herself in the third person and as part of the landscape. At this point, she is so much the natural child that it is hard to tell where nature ends and she begins; she comments,

"I had grown up untrained and merry-hearted, like the willows by the stream" (34). The premise of the novel, however, is that at this point—despite having reached the age of maturity—she has not actually grown up. For that she will need to be removed from this wild natural environment and sent to the city. This journey is instigated not by her age, but by her grandmother's death (she has lived in the woods with her grandmother and her nurse, Ilse, since her mother's death). Once the grandmother dies, Ilse decides that Lenore deserves a proper education and writes to tell the girl's father that she is bringing Lenore to the city. Ilse is aware of what is lacking in Lenore, even if Lenore does not see it for herself, and insists on bringing the "child" to her father in the city:

> Once for all, the child shall not run wild on the moor! Look at Lenore! She can hardly read; as for her writing,—Lord have mercy on us!—you should see what work she makes of it. She can climb trees, and peep into birds' nests, but not a decent stitch can she sew, or knit a row upon a stocking; all I could do I never could teach her. (96)

While Ilse's concern is with practical skills, the novel's concern extends beyond these matters to moral ones: the ability to know whom to trust, how to speak with integrity, and how to make the choice of a mentor and a husband.

In the city, Lenore's wildness becomes even more pronounced in contrast to the civilization around her. She is described (with racial overtones I discuss in chapter 4) as a "little black creature" with "dark elf-locks" (106). She is embarrassed by both her darkness and her clothing; in one passage, she tells us: "I looked down at my shoes, as they sprawled their clumsy proportions upon the gravel, and then I pulled at the skirt of my black dress, to lengthen it, if I might, by even a fraction of an inch" (89). In the city, her perspective changes—now the standard of behavior is not her comfort but the opinions of others, and those others clearly are both attracted to her wildness and amused by her lack of polish. Upon first interacting with a group of young people in the city, she laments, "If I had been standing in the pillory, my shy face could not have worked and flushed more painfully than it did, exposed to the fire of all those strange, curious eyes" (89). This sense of mortification pushes Lenore to consider herself in a new light, and at this point, she does not like what she sees. Dagobert Claudius, who had first seen her on the moor and who owns the city estate where her father lives and works, is surprised to see her in the city. Laughing, he exclaims to his friends: "The little moorland Princess I told you about!—the barefooted little creature that slipped through the heather like a lizard,—a lizard, to be sure, with the Princess's crown!" (89). Transplanted from the moor where she reigned as "princess," dressed up in her nurse's idea of proper city clothes, with a black dress and heavy shoes, Lenore has regressed rather than progressed. However, the pain of these interactions starts her on a different path—one that suggests life in the city might actually be more than something to be endured.

Unusually for Backfisch novels, Lenore is not sent away from parents but to her father, whom she has not seen since she was three, when her mother died. While contact with her father begins her transformation, he in no way serves as a mentor for her. In fact, one of the challenges Lenore faces is that it is not immediately clear who is to teach her to be a woman. Many people might fill that role, but her first choices of models quickly prove to be inadequate and even detrimental to her education. In many ways, this novel is more complex than other Backfisch books.[4] While it takes the basic plot of a Backfisch story—a brief period in the life of an adolescent girl, a journey from home, an education that results in marriage—it also addresses issues of race, class, and religion at more sophisticated levels than is typical of other examples of the genre.

While Gretchen's task is to learn to follow the rules, which are clearly laid out by her aunt, Lenore needs first to choose a mentor whom she can trust to help her discern which rules are the right ones in a world of intrigue and contradiction. The contrast between her familiar world of the moor and her new life in the city pushes Lenore into a liminal space where suddenly she finds herself asking new questions and stirred by strange feelings, "ponder[ing] upon matters that had always seemed quite natural and commonplace" (33). Social interaction, rather than the natural progression of growing older, triggers her growth into womanhood. Full of fairy tale references, the novel hints that Lenore herself is a fairy-tale princess. Without the figurative kiss of the social world, she could have remained a natural child, asleep to anything but her physical experience of the wild moor for her entire life.

As with Gretchen, Lenore's most important lesson is learning to make good choices. However, while Gretchen's choices are clearly laid out for her, and her biggest hurdles are forgetfulness and a lack of care, the gothic nature of *The Little Moorland Princess* leads Lenore onto more dangerous ground. Is she to delight in the beautiful Charlotte or shrink from her unstable character? Is she to rejoice in being reunited with her aunt Christine or recognize the falseness behind the painted façade? Is she to see Claudius as a mentor or a murderer? The clear-cut world of the Backfisch as Gretchen experiences it is muddied for Lenore, but in the end, the consequences are the same. With the right choices come happiness; with the wrong choices—as her Aunt Christine models—come poverty, an impoverished mind, and loneliness.

As with Gretchen, Lenore's first struggle is with her appearance. When Lenore moves to the city, her "brown feet" are shod in heavy shoes by Ilse as a nod toward bourgeois practicality, a move that makes Lenore seem awkward and clumsy. When her new companions in the city replace these shoes with fairy slippers, and her grandmother's mourning dress with a white dress that liberates her, she comments: "My light draperies floated about me as if I were enveloped in a fleecy summer cloud" (183). In a metaphor rather obviously conveying the novel's vision of feminine transformation, she emerges as a result of this wardrobe change as a "butterfly" (184). Several contrasting scenes in which Lenore sees herself literally reflected also reveal her profound alteration. On the moor, Lenore's mirror was a pool where she frightened herself by imagining that the eyes she saw there were those of a goblin. When, dressed in black, she first sees herself in a real mirror, she does not even recognize herself. Later, dressed in clothing suitable to her age and form, she suddenly likes what she sees in the mirror: "I cast a glance towards the mirror, and suddenly discovered that my hair, that had always been to me an abomination, curled in really charming short black curls, and contrasted wonderfully well with the white ribbons of my hat" (189). This novel complicates a simple transformation from unformed Backfisch to civilized young woman by first emphasizing Lenore's wildness, then replacing it with her nurse's version of "civilized" dress that oppresses her and makes her the object of ridicule, before presenting a third option—the clothing that allows her to feel her free childish nature while also displaying herself as the product of culture. The natural self becomes clothed in expensive shoes and dresses and is adorned by the priceless pearls she inherited from her Jewish grandmother.

Lenore becomes pretty before she becomes civilized, and this alteration of the physical self is only the prelude to the real education and transformation she needs. The *Little Moorland Princess* is full of hidden staircases, locked doors, and secrets. Lenore's entrance into city life is also an introduction to deception: "Scarcely entered upon my new existence, I already had something to conceal from those around me,—I whose thoughts and speech had hitherto been as free and unconstrained as my floating hair in the moorland breeze" (140). The urban setting in which maturation must take place requires a guide, but will that guide lead Lenore to an inner life that oppresses or liberates her? Her choice of mentor is an emotional rather than a rational one. While her nurse Ilse immediately trusts Claudius, Lenore spends much of the novel believing the stories others tell about him and shrinking from his presence. As her fantasies about other potential mentors are shown to be false, and as Lenore finds herself strangely attracted to Claudius and even in love with him, she begins to act for his approval rather than for the approval of others.

Thus Lenore's first struggle is to be open to her own education. Shortly after she arrives in the city, she finds a pool in the garden outside her home and once again enters a body of water. This time, she is repulsed by her feet "that had, to [her] disgust, already grown whiter from their few days of close confinement. It was as if all the new-forged fetters fell from body and soul at the touch of the water" (153). As long as Lenore sees her education as a set of "fetters" rather than a ladder to new pleasures and herself "as insignificant as a floating piece of thistledown between two oaks," she is confounded (117). But by the end of the novel, she chooses for herself—while others decided to send her to the city, now she claims her own future, making the decision to educate herself into a useful woman with language that is reminiscent of Jane Eyre: "I did not go to bed that night; I seated myself upon the low window-sill and awaited the dawn. The day that began to glimmer faintly behind the treetops should usher in a new life for me" (292). The next morning, she walks through the woods to enroll herself as a student.

Unlike Gretchen, whose spiritual and moral life is in order before the novel begins and who must simply learn to make her outer self the appropriate vessel for her good nature, Lenore is introduced to us as amoral—more like a willow tree than a human being—and as quickly tainted by the evils of city life. Her task is to redeem herself, to grow toward an inner self that matches her beauty, and to develop a sense of integrity and self-worth. Self-discipline is a key tool in her education, and its success is marked by the fact that she does not lose her wild nature but simply subordinates it to her reason. She tells Claudius,

> "It has gone hard with me, I don't deny it, but I have conquered myself."
>
> "Indeed!" The same smile flitted across his face. "You have entirely abjured, then, all the moorland habits? You despise climbing trees, and cannot understand how you could ever wade in the water."
>
> "Oh, no, I am not so far as that by a long way!" I exclaimed, in spite of myself. "Indeed, I cannot believe that the time will ever come when I can hear the rustling of the trees and the merry rippling of the brook without longing; but I will learn to control the longing, just as I have compelled myself, against my nature, to write thus." (301–2)

Lenore refers here to her struggles with handwriting and the transformation of her "black, sprawling letters" into elegant copperplate (145). Like Gretchen, she has shaped herself into a woman worthy of being the wife of the man she loves, and she has done so not by leaving her childish self behind but by subjecting it to rigorous self-control. The "large eyes" that began the novel staring into a pool to see herself reflected in nature now turn to Claudius for another reflection of self—as a woman and a wife (384).

These two early examples of the early German girls' novel lay out a common structure: both portray a journey away from home that turns the natural heroine into an awkward adolescent, newly self-conscious and aware that she needs self-improvement. These examples also point to the diversity in the Backfisch novel, which typically relies on domestic realism but also sometimes integrates sensational elements. While the Backfisch novel has often been read as inscribing cultural norms upon the girl protagonist, these examples help us to see that the Backfisch's transformation is also the result of her own choices. The model of successful womanhood may be culturally determined, but in the context of a community and text that value the space of her education, a girl can effect her own successful maturation.

By highlighting the girl's awkwardness rather than her perfection, by recognizing the significance of a *Backfischzeit*, and by making the girl's transformation into adulthood desirable, the pattern laid out in German *Backfischliteratur* brings best-selling American adolescent novels of the same period into sharper focus. Such novels include forgotten best sellers such as Prentiss's *The Flower of the Family* (1853) and A. D. T. Whitney's *Faith Gartney's Girlhood* (1863) as well as undertheorized books such as Alcott's *An Old-Fashioned Girl* (1869) and Susan Coolidge's *What Katy Did* (1872). These novels stand in contrast with books like Charlotte Mary Yonge's *The Daisy Chain* (1856), Alcott's *Little Women* (1868), or Margaret Sidney's *Five Little Peppers and How They Grew* (1881), which focus on the development of the family unit and sibling relationships rather than on an individual protagonist.[5]

While *Little Women* is often seen as the first American girls' book, I suggest that the genre begins earlier, with a novel that focuses on a single protagonist rather than on her family. Prentiss's *The Flower of the Family: A Book for Girls* was published in 1853 and translated into German in 1875. It tells the story of Lucy Grant, the second and most competent daughter of ten children, and her struggle not just to do the right thing but also to feel the right way. Lucy is a "fresh and simple" child with "a peculiar charm and attraction about her" and is singled out for "that sunny flood of luxuriant hair that shone around the sweet face, and the large, brown eye, rare in color as it was in size" (117, 308, 140). The narrator says of the "sensitive" and "dreaming" Lucy that "no stranger could have met the child in her wanderings, or seen her sitting thoughtfully by the fireside, or watched the grave face she wore at church on Sundays, without marking and holding her in long remembrance" (27). In fact, the man she ultimately marries falls in love after a single glance and waits decades for her on the strength of that first impression. Like the much later Rebecca in *Rebecca of Sunnybrook Farm* (1903), she stands out from her siblings; she was "worth a dozen of [her older sister]" (12). Lucy quickly learns all the village school has to teach her and becomes the main support to both her parents. However, she is also a "fretting" and "gloomy" child, who complains about the "troubles" she faces: "We are so poor; and the boys are so noisy; and I can't go to school; and a new baby comes so often; and it tires me when I think it will always be so" (15, 10). She is fifteen when the novel begins and much older when it ends, but the focus of this story is on the two years in which she shifts from being a daughter who resents the demands of domestic life to the cheerful "sister-mother" on whom "all the household care descended" as her mother becomes ill and eventually dies (348).

Lucy's experience of adolescent uncertainty is described first by her father, who tells her, "We have watched you too long, and with too much solicitude, not to perceive that old things were passing away and all things becoming new" (24). Lucy's interior turmoil is soon reflected in a shift in physical space when she travels to the city to stay with her aunt, uncle, and cousins. Here she experiences the awkwardness of being a country cousin whose clothes are not right and who is unused to society manners. On her first night in the city,

> She was heartily glad to find herself soon advised to retire for the night, for she felt not only weary, but embarrassed and annoyed.... [at] the contrast between her own country style and that of the city.... She had read of "country cousins," whose air, and speech, and raiment

all conspired to make their city friends blush for very shame; and how did she know that she had not fallen into the same error? (100–1)

At home, Lucy had been able to construct a sort of peace for herself; she accepts that her family cannot send her to school, that her days will be filled with the work of tending to others, and that happiness comes from doing what is right rather than what is pleasant. The city presents new challenges and forces her to recognize that she has much to learn. Lucy exclaims, when unsure about how to behave in her uncle's home: "I never spent one hour from home before, and I always asked mother what I should do, and she always seemed to know!" (124). The solution to Lucy's sense of being unmoored is to turn to God: "The fitful temper wanted something whereon to fasten itself. The changeful humor yearned for something that knew not change. The distrustful heart must have a rock on which to plant itself" (134). On her sixteenth birthday, she experiences Christ as her "rock" and finds a new sense of peace (135). Living away from home and interacting with people who do not share her family's values allows Lucy to finish growing up, gives her a wider perspective on the world, and makes her realize what choices lie before her. Lucy's father defines this period in her life as a "necessary season of refreshment and repose" (167), acknowledging both her changing relationship to her community and the value of education. Lucy's loving family spares her and the labor she could contribute because they believe she deserves a self-centered time and space.

Lucy's story ends with the abrupt marriage that is typical of the Backfisch novel. We never actually see Lucy and her husband together after the brief moment when he first catches a glimpse of her at her brother's sickbed. When Lucy's father asks her, at one point, about the man who will become her husband, she replies simply, "I don't remember him," and "her father withdrew his questioning gaze, with a satisfied air, that said, 'She is a child still. How could I doubt it?'" (319). As this example powerfully illustrates, although these novels point to adolescence as a time when "old things become new," they do not acknowledge that this transformation is in part sexual. This story finds a kind of closure in marriage, but the protagonist's real reward and triumph are those of character: "Lucy was satisfied with being unknown, with the 'trivial round, the common task,' with the sweet rewards of home-affection, and the approbation of a conscience at peace with God. What would be the worth of the highest honors of this world without these?" (362). Lucy's success is not only social—marriage—but also spiritual.

The Flower of the Family was reprinted as late as 1999 and has had particular appeal among Christian homeschooling families. If we assume the girls' book must be either a family story or an orphan girl book, it appears to be an anomaly. However, with the model of the Backfisch novel before us, *The Flower of the Family* becomes not simply a moral tale of feminine Christian virtue but also a clear commentary on the "problem" of female adolescence and the need for a protected space for growth. Lucy's story is as much about the difficulties of becoming a woman as it is about her spiritual success. Because she moves from one loving home to another and is provided with a variety of mentors, her energy can be aimed toward self-improvement rather than survival.

These three examples of early adolescent novels for girls help us see that Alcott's *An Old-Fashioned Girl*—the Backfisch novel best known to English-language readers—is distinct from Alcott's family stories and engaged in a tradition of adolescent girls' fiction. The first seven chapters of the novel were serialized in *Merry's Museum* in 1869, and the novel was published in 1870 with an additional twelve chapters. (A German translation in two volumes appeared in 1872.) The first section describes Polly, the titular "old-fashioned girl," and has much in common with later orphan girl books; Polly is an engaging girl who helps transform those around her without really changing herself.[6] However, in the second part, which begins six years later, she is more like the Backfisch heroine. She needs to be transformed, to take on a different role in her community, and she is rewarded for her transformation with marriage.

Polly's physical appearance is a constant throughout both parts. She is introduced in Part One as a "fresh-faced little girl" with a "half-shy, half-merry look in her blue eyes" (4). Her exuberance and her attempts to mind her manners are both typical of the heroines of girls' novels: "Polly gave a little bounce on the springy seat, and laughed like a delighted child.... composing herself the next minute, as if it suddenly occurred to her that she was going a-visiting" (5). She has "pretty brown curls" and a way of putting Tom, her young host, at ease (6). She is a playful girl with womanly manners. At the beginning of Part Two, she is "bright-faced," and "the blue eyes were clear and steady, the fresh mouth frank and sweet, the white chin was a very firm one in spite of the dimple" (148–49). Her health is shown to be the cornerstone of her beauty, and her active life the cause of this health. In contrast, the women around her see themselves as too elegant to work. Through their idleness, they become fatigued and worn, even turning into invalids.

In the city home of the wealthy Shaws in the first part, Polly quickly feels the gap between herself and these city friends. Within moments of reuniting with her friend Fanny, Fanny admonishes her for showing enthusiasm for her beautiful bedroom. Fanny explains that "the other girls" will "laugh at everything the least bit odd" (8). Learning that "odd" is code for "countrified" makes Polly feel "uncomfortable" (8). Although from Fanny's perspective Polly needs to suppress references to her own home to be comfortable in the city, the novel shows that Polly's country education is in fact what leads to her success.

The virtues of Polly's lack of urban sophistication become clearer when, despite having accepted confining social expectations, she breaks free and enjoys a sledding session with some little girls. Fanny, horrified, explains that this was "horridly improper" and that she would "be mortified to death" if her friends had seen Polly (46). The hyperbolic "mortified" followed by the redundant "to death" highlights the limits of Fanny's education. What actually is deadly, the novel suggests, is Fanny's life of dissipation and lies, not Polly's wholesome country clothing and manners. Thus, in this novel, even Polly's awkwardness of dress and manners are markers of her success rather than qualities in need of reform. Fanny's grandmother rebukes a society that allows "children" to "lead idle, giddy, unhealthy lives, and get *blasé* at twenty" and celebrates Polly's old-fashioned version of adolescence (13).

The liminal space of Part One of this novel, the "new world, ... where the manners and customs were so different from the simple ways at home," makes Polly feel like a "stranger in a strange land" (37). It is clear that Polly's experience in this strange land benefits not her but those around her. Her return home is joyful, a return to "loving faces" and values that do not make her feel awkward and uncomfortable (144). This heroine is not in need of transformation, but encourages a nostalgia for old-fashioned values and clothing. The Polly of Part One is a representative of idealized girlhood, a positive example who helps those around her live better lives. She seems confident of her role and her ability to feel happy while creating happiness for others. The narrator tells us, "Insignificant as she was, she yet might do some good," and "She made sunshine for herself as well as others" (50, 56). Polly remembers her mother saying, "Even a little girl could exert an influence, and do some good in this big, busy world," suggesting that due to her upbringing she is already completely educated (142–43).

There are, however, moments in Part One that suggest that new complexities are in Polly's future. At the end of Part One, she writes in a journal that she wants to go home because "there isn't any one to help me get right when I get wrong" (84). She decides that the problems she faces in this city household are "my fault a good deal" and resolves to be "patient and pleasant," "good and grateful ... for I want them to like me, though I'm only 'an old-fashioned country girl'" (85). Such comments give us insight into a hidden side of Polly's experience: the darkness that lies beneath the "sunshine" of her demeanor. These words suggest that she is still in need of education—not the "fashionable school" where Fanny goes to waste her time but another kind of experience in the world (8). The work Polly does to overcome the tension between her desire to do right and her desire to be liked, the desire to be of use and the desire for luxury, are the subject of Part Two. Now the protagonist does need to do the work of transforming herself. As a woman of twenty, Polly should be ready to take on an adult life; she is no longer "an old-fashioned country girl." While those around her anticipate she "will make a charming little woman" as she has "a sensible mother," her task is to go beyond the lessons she has learned from her mother and make her own choices about the kind of woman she will be (136).

Part Two begins six years after Part One, with a Polly who leaves home again and who now must make the transition from girlhood to womanhood; she is twenty rather than fourteen, self-possessed rather than awkward, but she is still a "shy, sensitive girl" (213), who fears ridicule and struggles with going among strangers (167). Although she feels that her only option is to wait until she is "as old and homely, and good and happy, as Miss Mills [her landlady]," the novel suggests otherwise (177). The novel shows that Polly can in fact be young and good, moral and happy—but she must be willing to take chances, to make herself vulnerable to ridicule, and to take advantage of the growth a *Backfischzeit* offers. In language that anticipates Hall's image of the "budding girl," the narrator of *An Old-Fashioned Girl* describes the *Backfischzeit* with a botanical analogy:

> Polly had reached that point where the girl suddenly blooms into a woman, asking something more substantial than pleasure to satisfy the new aspirations that are born; a time as precious and important to the after-life, as the hour when the apple blossoms fall, and the young fruit waits for the elements to ripen or destroy the harvest. (213)

Although Polly is unaware of the significance her choices will have for her future, Miss Mills is able to push her toward a useful rather than purely decorative life. Like Gretchen in *Gretchen's Joys and Sorrows*, who learns that education "nips in the bud all wrong and pernicious influences" (93), Polly learns that growing up doesn't just happen, but must be learned.

Polly's first winter in the city is a difficult one, but it is one that plants "the seed of new virtues" (228). For Alcott, the work of womanhood is not simply domestic and moral but also practical and artistic. Alcott's novel relies on the standard courtship plot to advance the narrative, however, and Polly's two romances allow us to see both her need for further development and her successful transformation. The first, with Mr. Sydney, provides an example of error; her flirtation, as harmless as it seems, does real damage: "She only meant to have a good time, and there was no harm in that; but, unfortunately, she yielded to the various small temptations that beset pretty young girls, and did more mischief to others than to herself" (249–50). The allure and danger of the Backfisch are linked—her artlessness makes her desirable, but her lack of maturity or consideration of consequences can ruin friendships and lead to expectations that will not be fulfilled.

Polly's second romance is the result both of her own successful transformation and the transformation of the man she has cultivated: "the loving heart that had always seen, believed, and tried to strengthen all good impulses in Tom, was well repaid for its instinctive trust by the happiness of the years to come" (377). Here *An Old-Fashioned Girl* distinguishes itself from other girls' novels of the period in which a husband appears ready-made. By suggesting that both Polly and Tom need to grow up to create a happy partnership, Alcott sets the stage for a model of the girl as an agent of transformation. Rather than simply becoming worthy of reward, the work of womanhood also encompasses shaping those around her.

The Backfisch novel focuses on the girl's own innocence within a protected community. The adults around the Backfisch—who is sexually mature but not psychologically ready for marriage—protect her against inappropriate male attention while preparing her for a sanctioned relationship with a man. In contrast, later theorists of adolescence focus on the dangers of adolescence and the erotic appeal of the adolescent girl. Such theorists' definitions of adolescence allude to both the adolescent girl's desirability and lack of awareness of her sexuality. Hall's description of the category begins with an image that links the girl's innocence with sexual innuendo. He writes: "Girls with hair demurely braided down their backs and skirts just beginning to lengthen toward their ankles *are* buds that should not blossom for some time" ("The Budding Girl"). With the word "demure," Hall evokes both the girl's propriety and her potential coyness; by drawing attention to her lengthening skirts, he images for us what lies beneath these skirts. Hall's interest in the erotic appeal of the teenaged girl reflects a wider cultural perception; as Sally Mitchell points out in *The New Girl*, early definitions for "flapper" (an early translation of "Backfisch") mark the category as "quasi-mature: erotically attractive but not yet marriageable" (183). Similarly, Marah Gubar, in her study of Golden Age British children's literature, claims that "the most titillating figures are those who vacillate between innocence and experience, blurring the line between child and adult" (*Artful Dodgers* 178).

This is exactly the position occupied by the Backfisch, but in these early novels, we see the girl's own perspective rather than that of adults. Her story is thus about her own personal development. While the adults around the adolescent girl are aware of her bright eyes and her ankles, and may be anxious about the girl's sexuality, the girl herself is not. If we see the Backfisch from an outside perspective, we think about her as sexually attractive; if we experience her stories as she does, we see awkwardness and the need for growth and protection. Sexual vulnerability in these novels is actually the focus of the (male) reader or psychologist, not the concern of the heroine who is safe and who is focused on herself rather than on wanted or unwanted male attention. These are novels of personal transformation, not romance stories that foreground the girl's sexuality.

Natural, unspoiled girls, dressed up in city clothes by loving aunts and friends, these four country girls are examples for their peers and readers. These adolescent heroines all leave home to acquire a needed education, they all feel a sense of awkwardness, and they all are imagined by their authors as interesting and significant. While Gretchen learns to be clean and neat so that her outer appearance matches the interior virtue already in place, Lenore must learn to discern hypocrisy from love, Lucy is tried by domestic duties so that she can advance spiritually, and Polly's story emphasizes that a healthy community relies on socially engaged women. Within a shared pattern, the novels differ in the ways that they explore the complexities of girlhood within the protected space of a *Backfischzeit*.

A metaphor for the life of the mid-nineteenth-century adolescent girl in both Germany and America, the Backfisch helps us to see three key points. First, like the fish at the back of the boat, the teenage girl is in between roles. No longer a child but not yet old enough to be married, she exists in a state of anticipation, uncertainty, and shifting responsibilities. She leaves home to enter a liminal space that encourages change; this shift of physical space mirrors the psychological shifts at the core of each novel. The heroine's need to leave home and to deliberately engage in a maturation process emphasizes that while physical development may unfold naturally, appropriate social and psychological development requires determined effort and intention and the care of mentors.

Second, as the image of a flapping fish suggests, these heroines are likely to be less charming than their counterparts in later girls' novels. Like twentieth-century heroines, these early protagonists are healthy, loving, and eager to please, but they share a physical and social awkwardness that causes them embarrassment and shame. Whether the heroine is distressed by her unchristian behavior, her dirty gloves and runny nose, her family background, or her poverty, she is aware of the work of self-transformation that needs to be done so that she can move into a desirable state of successful adulthood.

Third, the limits of the Backfisch metaphor point to one of the most important messages that these novels consistently deliver. While the fish is at the mercy of the fisherman and cannot influence its fate, the Backfisch can use her own education and the opportunity of the *Backfischzeit* to assert some authority over her life. The Backfisch's future happiness depends not on her changing those around her but on changing herself. One reward for self-transformation is the ability to transform others, and the Backfisch learns in part by serving as a mentor to others. Ultimately, the heroine of the Backfisch novel becomes a model of domesticity and is rewarded with the perfect marriage.

An important early strand of the girls' novel emerges here, in a messy arena of unwashed faces, muddy boots, and awkward manners, but also in a profound search for social and spiritual identity. At the center of these stories is the liminal space that allows for rebirth as a woman—and in these novels the girl may choose the shape she will take. These novels frame her choices as moral ones, with high stakes, but also show her own agency as key in the process of becoming a woman.

These novels all present heroines who need to change (by moving past awkwardness), who are able to change (because of the opportunity offered by their protected liminal space), and who do change (and are rewarded by love and marriage). These girls are defined by their need of education, and they profit from the opportunity to experience the turmoil and awkwardness of adolescence. In a physical space beyond their family home, they are able to work toward a mature identity. Adolescence becomes defined as an uncomfortable but profitable time and space; the Backfisch story acts to define and protect the *Backfischzeit*. By naming the adolescent girl—the Backfisch—and the transformative period of adolescent girlhood—the *Backfischzeit*—these novels insist that the adolescent girl is both interesting and worth the investment of time and attention.

The protagonists' interactions with their mentors in these novels highlight a contrast between contemporary images of adolescence that rely on Hall's notion of adolescence as a "baffling problem" and the perspective of the Backfisch story, which suggests that adults can competently guide girls through adolescence. In her insightful essay "Toward a Theory of Adolescence: Queer Disruptions in Representations of Adolescent Reading," Gabrielle Owen argues that "we say that adolescents are confused, unstable, hormonal, rebellious, or uncertain in order to distance these qualities in ourselves" (121). What the Backfisch novel helps us see is that this distancing process and the abjection of the adolescent are not inevitable. Polly, adolescent in her search for identity, is neither disrespectful nor rebellious. Most significantly, the adults around her view her adolescence not as a problem, but as an opportunity. While Polly and other heroines are abject in their awkwardness, they are valorized for their transformative potential. The fact that adults can successfully educate adolescent girls makes them feel good about themselves and the girls they mentor.

By defining the Backfisch as endearing, awkward, and full of potential, mid-nineteenth-century adults were able to validate their own power to help the girl make good decisions and to successfully educate her. By turning to an earlier phase in the history of the adolescent (the story of the adolescent girl as described in the Backfisch novel) we can conceive of a different relationship to the adolescent—affection rather than abjection. These novels show us what it would be like to embrace adolescence and our own transformative potential rather than distancing ourselves from it.

By seeing the process of female maturation as a worthy literary subject, mid-nineteenth-century authors acknowledge the adolescent girl as a subject, impress upon readers the importance of the work she has to do, and create an imaginative space for powerful images of female adolescence. While these novels are certainly focused on the socialization of girls into femininity and rely on images of virtuous womanhood as asexual and self-contained, they also insist on the importance of the adolescent girl. The question these texts ask of us is how we can move toward less constricting notions of adult femininity while holding on to this idea of adolescence as a time worth investing in rather than simply enduring. These stories suggest that adolescence is a collaborative experience rather than an antagonistic one, a valuable period of self-reflection within an expanded social circle. In the next chapter, I look more closely at the relationships that support the Backfisch's development and the ways that romance is redefined as mothering rather than heterosexual partnering.

· CHAPTER TWO ·
The Romance of Othermothering

> I pressed the dear picture to my lips, and was quite beside myself with joy.
> (*Gretchen's Joys and Sorrows*, chapter 11)

That romance is a key element of the Backfisch book is hardly a surprise. Its heroine becomes aware of her own deficiencies and longs for a relationship that will secure her identity; the novel typically ends with her marriage to a man and the promise of future happiness in a family circle. And yet, while the superficial plot structure of the Backfisch novel looks like that of the heterosexual romance novel, in these books the romantic focus is on relationships between women. For example, the title of chapter 20 of *The Flower of the Family*, "Every Life Has Its Romance," is only peripherally that of Miss Prigott's unconsummated love for Lucy's father; in this novel it is her love for Lucy herself and desire for a daughter that leads her to build a new house, buy a new carriage, and propose (to Lucy). Gretchen's overflowing emotional attachments in *Gretchen's Joys and Sorrows* are directed not at a potential husband, but at the women in her life. In the epigraph above she presses a picture of her friend Marie to her lips; in a later scene she "kissed again and again the dear writing" of a letter from her mother (61).

Read as a heterosexual romance, the girl's journey appears to be one that prepares her for marriage; her identity appears to be defined by men, both legally and also sexually. And yet men are peripheral or absent in the Backfisch book, despite the genre's roots in conduct books written by men and in sentimental novels that propose a lover who is also a father figure. Rather than moving directly from her father's home to her husband's, the heroine of the Backfisch novel enters an intermediate space where she is encouraged to develop intimate relationships with other women and girls. What is surprising about these novels is their focus not on the story of the girl's developing relationship with her future husband, but on her emotional transformation in a community of women. The girl learns to nurture, a key part of her emotional transformation: it is her ability to care for others rather than her ability to attract a husband that marks her passage to womanhood. Biological mothers—whose identities are closely linked to the fathers of these adolescent girls—are also absent or in the background. The Backfisch novel characterizes female adolescence as devoted to emotional and intellectual growth that is guided by nonbiological mother figures, outside the structure of patriarchal families.

An important early model for this pattern exists in the first British novel for girls, Sarah Fielding's *The Governess: or, The Little Female Academy* (1749), where the girl's education is linked to the absence of a biological mother, to peer mentoring, and to storytelling. This novel sets up a pattern of educating girls within a female community that was replicated in the Backfisch book. The school setting of *The Governess* is organized around two female educators—Mrs. Teachum, a widow who is the director of the school, and Jenny Peace, a student who provides the most direct and successful mentoring of the other students. Jenny is further empowered through the instruction she receives from Mrs. Teachum, whose limited engagement with her students is offset by her construction of a space in which they can tell each other stories—from spiritual autobiography to fairy tales—and learn to interpret those stories correctly. The multiple forms of storytelling in *The Governess* suggest that any text can educate; the key is to put texts in a context that helps young readers know how to interpret them. Through telling, listening to, and analyzing stories, girls learn to make sense of themselves and to make good judgments about others. This model shows us that one purpose of education is to improve the girl's discernment, to help her learn to "read" those around her by teaching her how to interpret stories. Drawing on this tradition, the Backfisch novel emphasized its practical value in the moral education of girls. As in *The Governess*, storytelling becomes a key process in the Backfisch novel. Reading itself becomes a way of learning gender in that it models intimate connection between author and reader and provides examples of women living in nurturing community.

This chapter examines mothering in four nineteenth-century novels for girls to argue that mothering as a communal enterprise can provide an alternative to essentialist conceptions of motherhood.[1] In so doing, it demonstrates how the embodied intimacy of shared mothering challenges the assumption that heterosexual or spiritual romance will be the primary form of romance in a girl's life. Instead, the focus of the Backfisch's attention—her emotional connections, her gift giving, and her sense of finding a place in the world—are tied to relationships with other girls and women.

Mothering is a fraught topic for feminist critics who seek to avoid biologically determined understandings of the options available to women while also acknowledging the material experiences of women who give birth and/or raise children. In order to acknowledge that mothering is different for different women and varies over the course of a mother's life, it is crucial we look not to a single overarching theory of motherhood but begin with "specific instances of mothering in specific contexts," as Patrice DiQuinzio argues in *The Impossibility of Motherhood* (244). This chapter examines the communal nature of mothering in the Backfisch novel as a way of illustrating the complexity of mothering relationships.

The Backfisch's social position and life trajectory (unlike those of later adolescent protagonists) are unambiguous; she is expected to grow up to be a wife and mother. Within the framework of the girl's pursuit of a husband (and the children who may well follow), it would be easy to see mothering as simply a consequence of marriage and mothers as merely reinforcing patriarchal systems as they raise their daughters to replicate their own life journeys. Yet despite the conservative plot and its reliance on heterosexual marriage as the marker of a girl's successful maturation, there are two ways in which the story of the Backfisch pushes us to rethink both the options available to women and essentialist notions of mothering as biologically determined. First, the focus of these stories is not the courtship that leads to marriage, but a world of women and girls supervised by single, adult women who are financially, socially, and intellectually independent. Though the heroine's explicit goal may be a husband, she spends most of the novel with grown women who have happy lives without a husband or children. Second, the heroine's journey away from home (and her mother's care) allows her and the reader to see that mothering, a form of physical and emotional care linked to preparation for the future, can be provided by women who are not biological mothers. The concept of othermothering, based on the need to share the nurturing and mentoring of children, extends biologically rooted notions of motherhood and decenters heterosexual models of power in favor of community mothering and mentoring.

The nineteenth-century authors whose work I examine here—Elizabeth Prentiss, A. D. T. Whitney, Clementine Helm, and Emmy von Rhoden—provide alternate models of mothering beyond the relationship of a biological mother with her child that is taken from the experiences of many twentieth-century middle-class white women, assumed as the norm by some critics and critiqued by others. In her essay "Social Constructions of Mothering," Evelyn Nakano Glenn asks that we move alternate perspectives of mothering from the margins to the center and suggests that looking at the mothering practices of women of color is one way to do this (5). Patricia Hill Collins develops one such alternate model, the practice of "othermothering," which describes the experience of many Black communities in which children are mothered by a number of community members, only some of whom are biologically related.[2] The works I examine in this chapter describe the lives of white middle-class girls and women but do not center their stories on biological motherhood. Instead, the fictional worlds they create, like the communities of color Glenn and Collins describe, rely on communities of girls and women to mother children and each other.

Othermothering functions in three ways in the Backfisch novel, all of which suggest the relational and communal nature of identity: at a meta-level, as narrators take on a mentoring role with their readers; at a formal level, when the protagonist is sent away to another woman who takes on the responsibility of mothering her; and at an informal level, as girls learn to nurture and care for one another through physical care and storytelling. All three levels assume girls need more and different mothering than they receive from their biological mothers and that women who are not themselves biological mothers can mother by providing physical and emotional care.

Narrators as Othermothers

At a meta-level, we can see the authors or narrators of the Backfisch book as positioning themselves as mentors to an audience of girls approaching womanhood.[3] Many Backfisch books directly address such readers, either in the preface or with a first-person narrator. In the following two examples, the Backfisch novel explicitly acknowledges its own potential to serve a mentoring role—and the author's potential to serve as a mentor at a distance. First, from the preface to Whitney's *Faith Gartney's Girlhood*:

> I dedicate it, as it is, to these young girls, who dream, and wish, and strive, and err; and find, perhaps, little help to interpret their own spirits to themselves.
>
> I believe and hope that there is nothing in it which shall hinder them in what is noblest and truest.
>
> May there be something that shall lift them—though by ever so little—up!

Similarly, in Helm's *Gretchen's Joys and Sorrows*, the first-person narrator writes:

> What I still remember of my experiences in Berlin I will now relate to you, my dear friends. They are, indeed, very pleasant remembrances for me; and as the race of backfischchen still thrives and blossoms, there is, no doubt, one or another among them who sometimes feels quite as unhappy as I did, and may these lines serve to comfort and entertain her. (4)

We have two similar addresses here, written fourteen years apart, one American, one German. Both addresses to the reader point toward a shared female experience. Both take on one of the two othermother roles that are further developed by characters in each novel: the wise, single adult woman (in the case of Whitney's address) or the intimate friend (in the case of Gretchen the narrator). Whitney speaks to the reader directly as author of the novel and as a mentor. She makes it clear her audience is girls "between fourteen and twenty" in need of some sort of "help." They are vulnerable, and part of her task (and the task of the girls' book) is to leave out those scenes that might "hinder" the girls' growth. Her mothering role is protective as well as encouraging. She defines girlhood as a time in which they "dream, and wish, and strive, and err . . ." as they look forward to the future and in which they look inward "to interpret their own spirits to themselves." This is a preface addressed to readers who are in a state of being made and making themselves. The expectations are high; they are to develop what is noblest and truest in themselves. And the novel offers the potential to help in this process.

In *Gretchen's Joys and Sorrows*, the address to the reader comes directly from Gretchen, the narrator and protagonist of this first-person narration, who is representative of the peer othermother. It comes at the end of the first chapter, rather than as a preface, so readers have already gotten to know Gretchen as a teen and a character. At this point in the text we are taken out of the narrative to a point in the present, in which Gretchen is now an adult, able to look back and advise others. The affection of the address, "dear friends," implies the reader and narrator understand each other, that they have an intimate relationship that allows Gretchen the narrator to influence and reassure the reader. As Gretchen looks back on her past, she positions herself as sharing with the reader an intimate world of unhappiness and growth.

Importantly, neither address refers to the book as a "novel." From a German perspective, the nineteenth-century *Roman* or novel was a more grandiose genre, demanding of its reader complex interpretation and intellectual engagement. From an American perspective, the novel was still firmly linked to the sentimental novel, with its implication of dangerous emotional lability and imaginative excess. Instead, these authors provided stories and narratives that gently comfort and instruct. Significantly, the American book (*Faith Gartney's Girlhood*) focuses on the book's ability to support moral growth, while the German book (*Gretchen's Joys and Sorrows*) suggests the reader just needs a source of pleasure. Both imply a girl in this period from "fourteen to twenty" needs mothering beyond that which her biological mother can provide. These books both position themselves as providing some of that mothering, and they suggest other models of mothering the girl reader can reach for in her own life.

Mentors as Othermothers

These novels also provide examples of single women, either relatives or teachers, who serve as othermothers. Just as Louisa May Alcott provides alternatives to the "sour, spiteful spinster" in her essay "Happy Women" (205), single women in the Backfisch novel participate in a model that imagines ways for women to be useful with or without marriage. Single women (spinsters and widows) in the Backfisch novel value marriage, but they value their usefulness and moral purpose more. It is worth noting a distinction between the German and American texts. In the German novels, while a period of spinsterhood can help teach a young woman to be a good wife, ultimately the marker of her success is marriage, and successful othermothers are widows rather than old maids. The American novels, in contrast, provide models of spinster women who successfully mentor girls. In both cases, what is "reproduced," in Nancy Chodorow's language, is a way of tending and befriending that requires only peripheral marriage and childbearing.

Three of the four novels I discuss here include a plot centered on the protagonist's departure from home to live with a woman who is not her biological mother. This pattern mirrors the situation of many mid-nineteenth-century American girls; as Carroll Smith-Rosenberg writes: "In the process of leaving one home and adjusting to another, the mother's friends and relatives played a key transitional role. Such older women routinely accepted the role of foster mother; they supervised the young girl's deportment, monitored her health and introduced her to their own network of female friends and kin" (18). Like the twentieth-century communities of women of color Collins describes in *Black Feminist Thought*, mid-nineteenth-century German and American women relied on the support of other adult women to help raise their daughters. This social reality was reflected in novels of the period.

In the earliest of the American Backfisch books, Prentiss's *The Flower of the Family*, we are introduced to fifteen-year-old Lucy as "old things were passing away and all things becoming new" (24). Lucy's mother is loving but exhausted. She lacks the time and money to nurture Lucy to the extent she needs, and it appears Lucy is headed toward a life of drudgery and repression. Instead, Lucy's plot shifts when her mother's brother takes her away to his wife in the city to be cossetted and educated. Travel away from home relieves the heroine of the domestic grind; it also allows her to see how others live and the variety of choices there are to make.

Lucy meets Miss Prigott, a spinster woman and childhood friend of her mother, who imagines herself as Lucy's mother and ultimately offers to adopt her. In later Backfisch books, single women like Miss Prigott will be positive sources of both emotional and financial support. In this story, with its ties to the sentimental novel, Miss Prigott is a trial to Lucy rather than a solace. She constantly criticizes what she sees as Lucy's self-centeredness and "insufferable pride" (123)—to the surprise of both Lucy and the reader, for Lucy seems much more a paragon of female virtue than a child in need of discipline. On

Lucy's birthday, Miss Prigott dismays her by giving her several tracts and suggesting Lucy might want to consider becoming a Christian. Since Lucy already sees herself as Christian, this gift causes a painful identity crisis, as Lucy wonders if she has failed her parents and her God in this new community: "The longer she looked at herself, the more discouraged and wretched she became" (126).

In despair, Lucy turns to God: "Amid the multitude of her thoughts within her, the idea of God alone offered repose. To Him then she turned. To Him she confessed her capricious, changeful temper; her doubts, fears, mistakes; and besought Him now and once for all to fasten her to Himself" (135). In this passage, God offers "repose," a confessional, the solace of forgiveness, and a solid place to stand: attributes that are given to othermothers in later novels. This sounds much like the message of the sentimental novel, that real education comes from a relationship with God and that it is better to invest in that relationship than in any human one. But the presence of Miss Priggott, and her instigation of Lucy's embrace of God as mentor, hints at the way the classic girls' book will develop. In later Backfisch books, the idea of God as mentor recedes into the background as a human mentor helps solve what increasingly become social and domestic problems rather than spiritual ones.

Lucy herself first sees Miss Prigott in terms of "her disagreeable qualities," but later comes to "see that underneath them she has something good" (148). The girls' book as a genre makes a similar step as it moves from stereotyping spinster women as abrasive and unlovable (Aunt Fortune in *The Wide, Wide World* is a prime example of this model) to imagining the spinster as a mentor who is devoted, loving, and able to contribute directly to the education of a young woman.[4] The single woman who wants to be a mentor is only partially successful in *The Flower of the Family*; she reveals her own weakness rather than serving as a model of adult femininity. Later characters in the genre (such as Aunt Miranda in *Rebecca of Sunnybrook Farm*) return to this model of the old maid who is nurtured by a loving girl, but the novels in the discussion that follows add another pattern, that of the woman whose lack of a male partner and children empowers rather than stigmatizes her.

The benefits to an adolescent girl of being mentored by a woman who is not her mother become clear in novels such as *Gretchen's Joys and Sorrows* and *An Old-Fashioned Girl*. In *The Flower of the Family*, while Miss Prigott explicitly wants to convert Lucy into a professed Christian, implicitly she wants to convert herself into a mother and Lucy into her daughter. Miss Prigott expresses her desire for affection from Lucy: "'From the very first hour I loved that young girl!' she said within herself; 'and my foolish old heart hoped for love in return. So it is after fifty years' experience of life; I am still childish, still hopeful, yet still disappointed'" (164). Miss Prigott courts Lucy like a suitor; imagining a life where they live together like mother and daughter, she even buys a new house and furnishes a room for Lucy. Though Miss Prigott never suceeds in nurturing Lucy, Lucy does respond to Miss Prigott's need for love and learns to care for her. Miss Prigott reminds us othermothering can serve not only the protagonist but the othermother herself. Like later North American books such as *Rebecca of Sunnybrook Farm* and *Anne of Green Gables*, *The Flower of the Family* shows how the desire to express love can be framed as mothering rather than marriage. And while these early novels for girls tend to focus on the girl's own transformation, *The Flower of the Family* hints at a key element in later girls' books—the protagonist's ability to effect the transformation of adults.

Miss Prigott is too needy herself to be the "rock" Lucy searches for and that later Backfisch heroines will find in other women. While Miss Prigott fails as a mentor, she does push Lucy to begin her own mentoring journey, an important rite of passage for the Backfisch. With God's help—rather than the help of a spinster aunt—Lucy learns to serve and shape others. Lucy has "a peculiar charm and attraction about her" (308). In this novel, her desirability is linked to a close relationship with God; in later novels this religious component is less present or absent, leaving simply a sense of the protagonist's charisma that lies in her ability to inspire and feel affection. While the first of the American Backfisch novels shows its link to the sentimental novel with a focus on the girl's relationship with God, as the genre develops, the primary moral influence is the desire to please other women rather than to please God, and romance is expressed through the desire and ability to nurture.

The German *Gretchen's Joys and Sorrows* and the American *Faith Gartney's Girlhood* were both published ten years later, in 1863. Both explore the complex ways in which adolescent girls are mothered and mother. Like Lucy, Gretchen and Faith need to establish an independent identity away from home. Their mothers are too tired or lack the knowledge their daughters need. Just as the Backfisch story accepts that adolescent girlhood is a messy work in progress, it acknowledges mothers cannot be all things to all people. Gretchen's mother is worn down by "many children and much sickness" (3) and Faith's mother "had not been strong for years" (120). Significantly, these mothers are not depicted as absent or morally lacking; they simply don't have the skills or energy that will allow them to help their daughters develop into their full potential. Rather than criticizing mothers for not being able to provide everything their daughters need, these novels suggest mothering is a shared enterprise. Gretchen's mother is honored as having provided a solid foundation that gives Gretchen a "childish cheerfulness" and "the quiet, domestic virtues upon which the happiness of her home was founded" (3).

> Her teachings formed the foundation of all that I learned in after life, and through them my heart and understanding received their early development. But my mother well knew that I could nowhere better receive the additional instruction that I so much needed, than at the hands of Aunt Ulrike, for she herself sincerely honored her excellent, highly educated sister-in-law. (3)

Gretchen's and Faith's mothers recognize their inability to teach their daughters all they ought to know; they encourage them to be mothered by another woman. As we read in *The Flower of the Family*, "All the mother's wisdom fails to supply to her child the place of [sic] that each must acquire for herself" (118). As these girls move into the transformative space of adolescence, they need to be in a physical space that balances the education they have received from their biological mothers with other perspectives and skills. While Gretchen goes to the city for her education and Faith moves to the country with her family, both are taken in hand by aunts who are themselves single, independent, successful women and who are able to othermother through love and mentoring.

As *Gretchen's Joys and Sorrows* opens, Aunt Ulrike is described as "motherly" (1) and "a motherly friend" (3). We learn later she is a widow and she misses her husband (39). She is clearly a mentor who will advocate for marital bliss, though she herself seems to be quite content with her independent life, full of friends and with financial independence. The shift from the early figure of Miss Prigott, whose desperate neediness sends Lucy closer to God, to the later Aunt Ulrike, whose calm confidence leads her to take on a God-like role in Gretchen's life, reveals the potential power of the single woman as mentor. Aunt Ulrike is both mentor and othermother; she combines training for life as a woman in society with emotional and physical support. Even the language Gretchen uses to describe Aunt Ulrike mirrors that which Lucy uses as she finds comfort in God. When Aunt Ulrike tells Gretchen her cousin Eugenie will be joining their household, Gretchen worries she will be neglected in the shadow of this new member of the family.

Aunt Ulrike reassures her: "'Have no fear my child,' said she softly; 'you shall suffer no loss through our new comer. I shall stand by your side to help and protect you, and my love will support you when it is necessary. Only trust to me, and be of good cheer'" (41). Gretchen's response could as easily be addressed to God. Indeed, in speaking of God's ability to know her thoughts, God's role as a confessor, and God as comfort and refuge from fear and embarrassment, her response echoes key phrases from Lucy's prayers.

> It was as if she had read all the fears of my poor heart; for without my speaking a word she seemed to know how weak and fearful I had been. Blushing deeply I now confessed my egotistical thoughts to her, and took good heart for all that might come, trusting full in her who had so often been my comfort and refuge. (41)

Aunt Ulrike also takes a God-like role in establishing guidelines for Gretchen's behavior; she "begin[s] at once to call attention to these things which she wished me to change" (8). Gretchen seeks to improve herself to please Aunt Ulrike rather than God.

The first thing Gretchen must learn is that being away from home marks a change in her status. Aunt Ulrike makes a clear distinction between the freedom allowed a child and the responsibilities that come with womanhood: "Children are allowed to do many things; but you are here to learn what is proper for grown persons, and to lay aside children's shoes" (8). Writing from the perspective of many years of experience later, Gretchen tells us that Aunt Ulrike "instructed me with care and faithfulness in the quiet, domestic virtues upon which the happiness of her home was founded, and never in my life can I sufficiently thank her for it" (3). While Gretchen's education includes proper comportment for social calls and balls, the focus of the novel is on creating a system that keeps your fingernails clean and your guests comfortable. The novel suggests these rituals of daily life will lead to happiness and successful participation in community.

Faith Gartney's Girlhood is another story of finding a community; it expands the horizons of the story with double heroines and double mentors. The Backfisch of the novel is Faith Gartney, the well-loved, white, middle-class girl, whose story begins the novel. But the novel also tells the story of Glory, an orphaned Irish girl, whom readers discover working for her keep in a home where she is not appreciated and certainly is not mothered. While Glory yearns to be part of a family and to love and be loved, Faith longs for productive work and purpose. Both despair that there are, in Glory's words, "such lots of good times in the world, and she not in 'em!" (139). Significantly, the novel argues the desire for "good times" is as legitimate for an Irish orphan as it is for the daughter of an old Connecticut family. As this novel defines it, being in the "good times" requires finding meaningful work, the work God has in mind for you and mentors can help you embrace.

The challenge is in interpreting the nature of that work when there is such temptation for women to self-sacrifice through a marriage or work that doesn't actually support their growth. The narrator writes: "Women's necessity is to lose herself—to give herself away . . . there are hundreds—thousands—like Faith Gartney, who marry from a pure, blind reaching for a holy sphere of good. They have entreated God to lead them. They have given up self and sought His work of Him" (225). But the novel makes it very clear the search for work does not justify self-abnegation. When we first meet Glory, she is working for an abusive employer who refuses her the pleasures of letting her hair grow or watching the party next door through an open window; this woman defines Glory as a drudge whose only purpose is to labor and fails to appreciate the ways Glory is loving toward her own children.

An old apple-selling woman in the park tells Glory the story of the little red hen who must use her wits to save herself by cutting out the bottom of the sack in which the fox has put her. It is Glory's responsibility to act, to save herself from abuse, as it will be Faith's responsibility to refuse marriage to a man who is not her equal. Faith and Glory learn these lessons not in church or prayer, but through the guidance of single women. The narrator writes: "God leads some through life toward Himself, as a mother wins a child, making its first feeble steps; with good held always in sight, and always out beyond the grasp" (175). Faith and Glory are led to their own mature identities by women who give them models of productive work and choice and encourage them to create family and community for themselves through that work, rather than defining themselves simply through their ability to please others.

While Faith's mother wants to protect her from domestic labor, Aunt Faith suggests "ugly" work may prepare the way for growth and describes the metaphor of cotyledons: "Two tough, clumsy, coarse leaves. . . . they'll last awhile, and help feed up what's growing inside and underneath, and by-and-by they'll drop off, when they're done with, and you'll see what's been coming of it" (136). She suggests viewing difficult tasks as leading toward God rather than as an end in themselves, but avoiding work that is simply drudgery. Aunt Faith and Nurse Sampson model a balance between self-indulgence and

Glory tells her orphan girls about Santa Claus. *Faith Gartney's Girlhood* (Boston: Houghton, Mifflin, 1892).

self-abnegation; they show us how it is possible for women to contribute while still nurturing individual identity.

It is through interactions with single women, who model independence, that these girls and the reader see the many options laid out before them. These options challenge the assumption that the only way to create closure in a girls' book is through heterosexual romance or that female success requires marriage. In *Faith Gartney's Girlhood* the narrator explicitly takes issue with the assumption in earlier domestic fiction that an unmarried woman must be a "scrawny, sour-looking old maid" and instead forces us to see Nurse Sampson in terms of her "decision, determination, judgment, and readiness" (73). While Faith's story becomes a fairly typical romantic story, Glory's does not (she never marries, yet othermothers four orphaned children); both end up with the feeling of being "in the good times."

In addition to mentoring and mothering Faith and Glory, Aunt Faith bequeaths both young women the financial means to do the work each has chosen. With this plot development, the Backfisch book takes a step further away from the sentimental novel, which links a woman's financial comfort to marriage. Aunt Faith invests in Faith and Glory and their work in the world; she enables and values their independence and independent purpose. She also acknowledges the pressures poverty brings to bear on mothering and the need for women to have the financial resources to nurture themselves and others.

The Backfisch novel imagines a world where the protagonist is nurtured by many adult women. In *Faith Gartney's Girlhood*, adult mentors give both Faith and Glory practical advice and resources that support them as they take on mature identities. In *Gretchen's Joys and Sorrows*, Gretchen learns from both her aunt and her new friend Marie how to maintain loving social connections. Unlike Jo in *Little Women* (a family story) or Ellen in *The Wide, Wide World* (a sentimental novel), these girls find mother substitutes who allow them to flourish outside of the family environment.

The Adolescent Girl as Othermother

The mothering behavior the protagonists of the Backfisch novel learn from their aunts and teachers translates into their relationships with their peers. While the final plot resolution comes with an engagement or marriage, emotional closure comes when readers see the heroine has learned to mother others, that she is herself a successful othermother. Historian Carroll Smith-Rosenberg explains that in nineteenth-century America, "Even more important to this process of maturation than their mother's friends were the female friends young women made at school.... one woman might routinely assume the nurturing role of pseudomother, the other the dependency role of daughter" (19). Smith-Rosenberg describes young women as going to absurd lengths to play these roles. The Backfisch novel provides examples of what Smith-Rosenberg calls "pseudomothering," though without the sense of absurdity Smith-Rosenberg describes. These protagonists are transformed into happy, satisfied women—with or without husbands—through the psychological and domestic labor that allows them to care for others.

For example, by the end of *The Flower of the Family*, Lucy will be glorified with the title "sister-mother" (348), a role the later Katy takes on in *What Katy Did*. We see her earning that title from the first pages of the novel: when the baby is hurt, only Lucy can comfort him; when her older sister is late coming home from school, Lucy takes on her domestic tasks; and when one of her brothers brings home strawberries, he splits them between his mother and Lucy with a smile. Gretchen othermothers her cousin Eugenie (helping her dress, modeling loving interactions) and is herself othermothered by her friend Marie (who eases her through the etiquette of her first ball and proper sidewalk manners). Faith's desire to do meaningful work is first recognized in her care for her brother when she takes over the work of the unsatisfactory nursery maid. "Kind, sisterly fingers helped Hendie now, in his morning robings; and sweet words and pretty stories replaced the old, taunting rhyme" (184–85). While Hendie's life clearly improves with the high-quality care Faith provides, the experience of mothering her young brother also has clear benefits to Faith.

In *An Obstinate Maid*, Ilse learns to othermother first by being othermothered by schoolmates. Her roommate, Nellie, helps her put away her clothes, teaches her to wash herself properly, and loves her unconditionally. Later, Ilse's love for a younger student, Lilli, leads her to finally learn to sew so she can make doll clothes for Lilli's doll. What is more, she nurtures Lilli and calms her on her deathbed. When Ilse returns home, she uses the skills she demonstrated in that relationship in caring for her newborn brother. All of these instances show mothering to be a diverse, communal project that extends beyond biological connection. And it is the ability to mother, rather than marriage, that is the topic of the Backfisch novel. While husbands may be scarce, as long as there is war, and poverty, and sickness, the work of mothering will be needed. Doing that work not only contributes to meeting the needs of the community but also transforms dissatisfied girls into productive, contented women.

"How perfectly lovely everybody is," said Katy, with grateful tears in her eyes. — PAGE 203.

"How perfectly lovely everybody is." *What Katy Did* (Boston: Little, Brown, 1910).

— 31 —

Ilse gab keine Antwort, sie fühlte sich so unglücklich, daß selbst der liebevolle Empfang der jungen Lehrerin kein Echo in ihrem Herzen fand.

"Möchtest du auf dein Zimmer gehen?" fragte diese.

Ilse nickte stumm, sie hielt noch immer das Tuch gegen die Augen gedrückt.

"Nellie!" rief Fräulein Güssow, "gehe mit Ilse hinauf und sei ihr beim Auspacken ihrer Sachen behilflich. Du

"Sie fühlte sich so unglücklich."(She felt so unhappy.) *Der Trotzkopf*, 68th edition (Stuttgart: Gustav Weise Verlag, n.d.), 31.

Men do appear in the Backfisch novel; in *The Flower of the Family*, it is Lucy's inept but loving father who first encourages her as she recognizes herself as undergoing a time of transition, and all of these novels achieve closure with the promise or description of a wedding. In contrast to the idea of the lover as father figure who instructs and mentors the heroine, lovers in these novels take on a range of peripheral roles and often appear only in a final chapter. Lucy's husband appears only twice in the novel; Ilse's future husband is first introduced in the last chapter. Susan Harris points out that "to attain 'full' rather than 'little' womanhood, the heroine of the sentimental novel must, if possible, marry well; specifically, genre conventions dictate that she marry a guardian of her morals as well as her person, often a 'dominating man'" (44). In contrast, while the Backfisch novel matches its heroine with a man of good character, he is not typically responsible for shaping her virtue. She must first learn from other women how to read character so she can make a good choice of partner. Both *Gretchen's Joys and Sorrows* and *Faith Gartney's Girlhood* use the choice of husband as a plot device; in both cases, the lover functions as a test of the girl's growing maturity rather than as a father figure or man to be saved.

The Story as Othermother

By the 1880s, the genre of the Backfisch novel was firmly established, and von Rhoden's *An Obstinate Maid* illuminates the ways themes of othermothering persist. While the protagonist Ilse's birth mother is dead, and it is her stepmother, Frau Anne, who fills the role of legal mother, Ilse calls her stepmother "Mama" and nowhere does the novel suggest her difficulties with Ilse result from a lack of biological connection. Rather, this novel helps us see the ways legal obligation—the formal role of mother, whether biological or not—interferes with the education of a daughter. Othermothers are effective largely because they mother without obligation; they choose willingly to love, educate, and nurture their otherdaughters.

Ilse leaves home because her parents confess themselves completely unable to educate her. Something must be done with this wild tomboy or she may someday be called "unweiblich" (unwomanly), a "furchtbar" (dreadful) thought (9). What is at stake here is not just Ilse's happiness and well-being, but also her parents' pride and the integrity of the community. Ilse's parents have a responsibility to send out a well-behaved young woman into the world. If they can't do it themselves, they must find someone else who can. In this case, the chosen method is a boarding school.

This is not simply a case of a divide between adult expectations and the idealization of childhood exhuberance[5]; Ilse's need for transformation is emphasized in her inability to fulfill her own desires. Despite her love of animals (the novel's initial conflict revolves around Ilse's desire to show her father some new puppies in the barn rather than dressing for dinner with company), she is too thoughtless to nurture the animals she loves effectively. For example, as Ilse packs her things to go to school, she puts a tree frog in a glass globe in her suitcase—and leaves it there for several days. She does include flies in the jar to nourish the frog, but the lack of oxygen results in a dead tree frog and more tears from Ilse. It is clear that left to her own devices, Ilse's impetuousness will only lead to sorrow, as "she had killed it through her own guilt" (54). She must learn to be more careful, to think through the consequences of her behavior, and to couple her intense emotions with discretion. She succeeds at school, despite the efforts of Fräulein Raimar, the director, who tries, unsuccessfully, to impose her will on Ilse, and in response to Fräulein Güssow, a young teacher, who succeeds in mentoring Ilse through a combination of love and storytelling.

In *Der Trotzkopf*, Ilse must learn the art of interpretation. But it is in what, specifically, she must learn to interpret that we see how the Backfisch novel reaches back to moral tales and distinguishes itself from the sentimental novel. As Trubey points out, in sentimental novels such as *The Wide, Wide World*, "'conversion' to proper womanhood ultimately is made possible not simply by reading the Bible, but by learning to read it *correctly*" (63). In *An

"Wie schlecht von mir, dass ich so dumm sein konnte!" ("How terrible of me, that I was so stupid!") Nellie comforts Ilse when she discovers that her frog has smothered. *Der Trotzkopf*, 68th edition (Stuttgart: Gustav Weise Verlag, n.d.), 54.

Obstinate Maid, in contrast, Ilse must study other girls' experiences. In this, the Backfisch novel reaches back to earlier moral tales and the idea of spiritual autobiography through a discussion of domestic life.

While, in general, the Backfisch book is less explicitly religious than the sentimental fiction that precedes it, American Backfisch novels retain more of a religious focus than their German counterparts. One American translator of *Der Trotzkopf*, Mary Ireland, underscores this distinction by adding Christian language to the text that is not present in the original and shifting some of the power of othermothering to God and away from the girl and her mentor.[6] For example, when Ilse storms to her bedroom to weep after being told she must go to school, her stepmother longs for the day when Ilse will recognize her love. The Ireland translation reads, "She could only lift up a prayer to God that her step-daughter might in time learn to love her who was trying to be a true and faithful friend to her husband's only child" (22). In contrast, the original German version states that Frau Anne "stayed behind and longed for the time when Ilse's good heart would help her find the way to her motherly love" (13). The original is more typical of the German Backfisch book, in which it is the girl's own "good heart" that is key, not God's grace.

In another example, when describing Lucie's transformation, the translation reads, "She learned to cast all her care upon her Saviour, and He gave peace to her soul" (108), while the original German simply states, "She went forward quietly and earnestly and her exuberant laughter disappeared" (80). In a third example, where Ilse has climbed the apple tree outside her window and harvested apples to share with her roomate, Nellie, the translation frames Ilse's remorse the next day through Christian notions of sin. Ilse says to Nellie: "In our Bible lesson, read last evening by Fräulein Bulow, were the words 'Thou shalt not steal'; what was I doing but stealing?" (130). In the original German, it is Ilse's own conscience that troubles her, without reference to external authority. Ilse feels ashamed for not having thought of taking apples as stealing, and her moral qualms define the situation for both her and Nellie. Ilse insists they must shake hands and agree they will never play a similar prank again.

Thus the American translation distracts us at several points from the ways the original German text embraces the notion of the Backfisch as othermother and the Backfisch's own moral compass. Ilse is most successfully mothered by young women—the young teacher, Fräulein Güssow; her friend Nellie—and even by the ridicule of other less-friendly schoolmates. After being corrected for improper table manners by the principal, Ilse storms to her room and insists she will leave the school. Her roommate, Nellie, calms her down: "Fräulein Raimar is right, she means well and isn't trying to criticize you. It's the same with all of us. We are young and dumb and need to learn" (43). While Nellie's perspective doesn't change Ilse's view of Fräulein Raimar, it does convince her to stay at the school, where her behavior is modified by a double program of the ridicule of her peers (especially around her table manners) and the loving compassion of Nellie and Fräulein Güssow. Ilse may not recognize her need for change, but the reader can see clearly that Ilse's current path will not be a pleasant one. Her "good heart" and lively ways seem likely to lead only to more tears unless she can somehow change her fundamental attitude. Ilse writes to her father, "I would so much rather have stayed at home; then I wouldn't know how stupid I am . . . I have learned only that I am very, very dumb" (58). This is perhaps significant progress and opens up the possibility Ilse will be able to learn something of use to herself.

The opportunity to learn comes with yet another battle with the principal, this one over the quality of Ilse's sewing. On the verge of being expelled for her bad temper, Ilse refuses to ask the school principal for forgiveness. She resists the advice of her young teacher and mentor until Fräulein Güssow shares the story of Lucie, who becomes engaged to a handsome artist, but then argues with him and fails to beg his pardon when she needs to. Fräulein Güssow warns Ilse that Lucie seemed "bent upon making him unhappy, the one whom she loved with her whole heart" (100). Lucie resists submission to both her fiancé and her grandmother; in her case, only time and regret effect a change.

This story-within-the-story marks a transformation point for Ilse: she finally realizes that if she can't master her own temper, she will be expelled from any loving community. By listening to a story about a girl her own age, told by a single woman only ten years older, Ilse is able to learn from someone else's experience. Neither Ilse's stepmother nor the principal (people in positions of authority) are able to help this willful girl grow into womanhood—it is her peers, a young teacher, and the power of the story and its correct interpretation that change her views. Ilse changes not to please God or to become a better Christian, but because she wants to be a harmonious part of the community of girls and women she has found at boarding school. Her "trotz," or obstinancy, can't be resolved with force or authority; it can be softened through affection.

At a key moment in *The Governess*, Jenny Peace reports to Mrs. Teachum that she has told the girls a fairy story, and Mrs. Teachum cautions her against too cavalier an approach to fantasy, saying:

> But neither this high-sounding language, nor the supernatural contrivances in this story, do I so thoroughly approve, as to recommend them much to your reading; except, as I said before, great care is taken to prevent your being carried away, by these high-flown things, from that simplicity of taste and manners which it is my chief study to inculcate.

Alone, the Backfisch is at risk of being "carried away" by the stories she reads and hears and by her own emotional experience and fantasies. With adequate mentoring—which provides both physical and emotional comfort and stability and instruction in the work of interpretation—the Backfisch will be grounded by love and held accountable to moral behavior. Like *The Governess*, the Backfisch books use stories within the story that may look like digressions but that can be interpreted to teach the protagonist how to shape herself. These layers of story assume a girl reader who in turn is being educated by the stories/protagonists at each level. By watching how the protagonist responds to hearing stories, the reader learns how to interpret the Backfisch book itself. As Ilse responds to Lucie's story, so should the girl reader of *Der Trotzkopf* respond to Ilse's story. In the telling of stories, the trials of adolescent girlhood are shown to be shared, strategies for emotional maturity are modeled, and a community of othermothering is formed.

Conclusion

Just as the narrators of the Backfisch book directly address readers—not as experts or authority figures, but as friends and peers—these characters help one another through stories that emphasize shared experience and challenges. Ilse's transformation comes not from reading the Bible and deferring to God, but from the physical care of peers, the story of another girl's life, and through her own opportunities to othermother. Though protective of biological mothers (they are generally good women who are loved by their daughters), these novels avoid essentialism and celebrate the individual's ability to function in a variety of roles as a loving and loved member of her community. While one perspective on the Backfisch suggests the awkward young girl must be polished so she is a suitable wife and ready to mother her own children, these stories focus instead on mothering within a world of women, where men are largely invisible and nonessential. The world is full of children and friends who need mothering; these novels suggest that, with or without biological children, the work of womanhood is to mother and be mothered. Ultimately, the "romance" that illuminates these texts is not a heterosexual romance or a Christian romance, but a romance of othermothering, as girl readers are led into a fantasy of female communities and intimate friendships without the distractions of husbands or children.

This narrative pattern is one that will become foundational for the girls' book. What Marah Gubar calls the "pleasures of female/female bonds" in the Anne of Green Gables series demonstrate one way twentieth-century girls' books are linked to their Backfisch ancestors ("Where Is the Boy?" 54). A world of women and girls can be a happy world, and narratives can successfully focus on romance between women with men at the periphery. We see pieces of this pattern as early as *Jane Eyre*, with Jane's relationship with Helen and, later, with her female cousins. In that novel, male lovers in the form of Rochester and St. John Rivers enter in as disruptive forces that shift our attention to possible heterosexual romances. The girls' book keeps the focus on girls and women.

In the twentieth century, the intense friendships that were considered normal in the nineteenth century are redefined as possible lesbianism, and thus, illness, as Laura Robinson points out in "'Sex Matters': L. M. Montgomery, Friendship and Sexuality." The residue of this prejudice, and a twenty-first-century focus on the dangers of inappropriate sexual touch, stand in stark contrast to the emotional and physical comfort girls and women provide for each other in the Backfisch book. One of the delights of Greta Gerwig's 2019 film adaptation of *Little Women* is the way the four sisters touch: they wrestle, tickle, caress, rest their heads on each other's shoulders. With this choice to show young women in close physical contact, Gerwig returns to a powerful nineteenth-century model.

Rather than limiting our reading of the early girls' book to its conservative plot structure, I propose we also consider what we can learn about healthy female adolescence from these portrayals of othermothering relationships. Backfisch novels help us see how early adolescent fiction resists two impulses that may damage adolescent girls. Instead of imagining the adolescent girl in terms of her sexual desirability to men, the Backfisch story provides models of emotional intimacy and interdependence that value the girl's own experience. And rather than assuming female growth requires the loss of maternal nurture, othermothering shows how the girl can stand between dependence and independence. Backfisch authors acknowledge the needs of nineteenth-century adolescent girls and show how reading can fulfill those needs. By acknowledging and embracing the confusing experience of adolescence for the girls they mentor, othermothers help construct a free space for exploration.

· CHAPTER THREE ·
Converting Girls into Women

One of the many responses to the 1860 translation of Charles Darwin's *The Origin of Species* into German was a series of lithographs published in the 1860s by Fr. Schmidt caricaturing Darwin's principles with images that show incongruous metamorphoses. Included in this series is an image that imagines the evolution of a fish into a young woman. This image works well as an introduction to this chapter, for it highlights the fraught question of transformation, the puzzle of how one thing becomes another. As Seth Lerer puts it, "Evolution, like imagination, lets us see how things turn into other things" (186). In the Backfisch story, the imagined transformation of a girl into a woman makes visible the effort and moral sculpting needed to shape a virtuous woman.

The Schmidt lithographs combine a theory of evolution with the imagination and take evolutionary principles to absurd extremes, moving from Darwin's narrative of apes coming down from the treetops and becoming human to images that show the shift from mosquito to elephant or cat to violin. The fifth lithograph in the series, "Enstehung eines Backfisches aus einem Backfisch" (Development of a Backfisch [teenage girl] from a Backfisch [fish]), draws on the notion that we move in utero through all the previous stages of evolution, starting as gilled creatures and developing into air-breathing mammals.

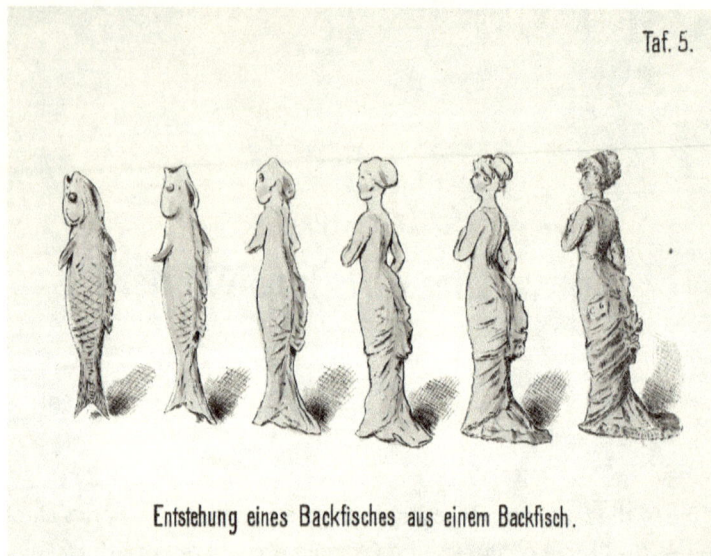

Entstehung eines Backfisches aus einem Backfisch.

Schmidt, Fr. "Entstehung eines Backfishes aus einem Backfisch." (Development of a Backfisch [teenage girl] from a Backfisch [fish]). *Evolution of household articles, animals etc. according to Darwin's doctrine*. Color lithographs by Fr. Schmidt, ca. 187-(?). Wellcome Library no. 680406i.

Starting with a carp posed upright on its tail, the lithograph presents a succession of six images that ends with a corseted and enculturated young woman. Both the images at the far left and far right include precise detail, while the image blurs as it moves toward the middle of the series, suggesting a moment of mystery in the translation of animal into human. Schmidt both relies on evolutionary theory (the watery origins of the human animal) and plays with a linguistic analogy (which equates the situation of the medium-sized fish with that of the teenaged girl). His image relies on humor and the unexpected visual overlap of fish and girl; it also suggests both creatures are social constructions.

Schmidt begins not with a fish undulating through water but with a carp perched precariously on its tail, posed deliberately, necessarily no longer alive. The girl, on the other hand, looks much like the idealized young woman found in a fashion magazine. By making the beautiful girl the evolutionary end of the dead fish, he brings her perfection into question. He shows the fish and girl to be parallel in outline, and also in that they are both removed from a "natural" state and manipulated for the purposes of art. The progression of images contrasts the idea of evolution as a natural process with a suggestion that identity is aggressively shaped. The title of the lithograph is also significant. While in a Darwinian context "Enstehung" is most appropriately translated as "evolution," the word also means "emergence," "birth," and "formation." The tension between the organic connotations of "birth" and the deliberate manipulation implied by "formation" points to a central concern of this chapter—the ways the Backfisch must be made into a woman rather than developing organically from childhood to adulthood. While the biological patterns of puberty suggest an inevitable maturation, Backfisch novels focus on the social construction of womanhood and the work this construction requires.

In this chapter, I use gender theory as a lens that helps us see the girl's transformation into a woman as a conversion experience. In this model, conversion is rooted in domestic labor rather than prayer; it is still infused with moral implications rather than an experience of organic growth. I rely on a theory of gender as a multipart structure to discuss two Backfisch novels—Clementine Helm's *Backfischen's Leiden und Freuden* (1863) (*Gretchen's Joys and Sorrows*) and A. D. T. Whitney's *Faith Gartney's Girlhood* (1863)—as well as Susan Warner's *The Wide, Wide World* (1850), a sentimental novel that provides helpful context.

Some girls' books begin with an already socialized heroine (*Pollyanna*, the Nancy Drew series); these books assume femininity to be essential and natural. Others lead unformed girls through the process of self-repression that leads to social approbation, exposing the work of becoming a morally successful woman. The latter type of girls' book—which I examine in this chapter—served as what Jane Tompkins calls a "training narrative" for girl readers by first acknowledging the hard work maturation requires and then providing a recipe for success (176). The explicit instruction provided by these novels also makes visible the ways "doing femininity" is a performance linked to the girl's desire for love and virtue.

The sentimental novel *The Wide, Wide World* draws its didactic power from the protagonist Ellen's failures more than her successes; her moments of weakness teach readers explicit lessons. As Ellen becomes more proficient in self-negation, her story moves more quickly—once she has learned to act and feel as a Christian, readers need only quickly skim ahead to the rewards of this self-control.

Like this sentimental novel, the Backfisch book focuses on the transformation of the subject. If this developmental arc is similar, the nature of the transformation is different: the focus here is on becoming a woman rather than on becoming a Christian. The Backfisch novel emphasizes the work of becoming a woman through a series of vignettes that show the heroine under duress. In this model, girls don't become women simply by waiting—they must act and fail, learn from their mistakes, and act again. While the reward for success is human rather than divine love, financial security rather than the promise of heaven, the moral urgency feels very similar in the two genres. These heroines don't become women "naturally" or effortlessly, nor is the acquisition of femininity morally neutral.

By aligning their plots with the conversion narratives laid out in novels such as *The Wide, Wide World*, Backfisch books make patterns of behavior that are intended to be interior and invisible, visible and teachable. When viewed through the lens of gender theory, Backfisch books also expose some ways the acquisition of gender was taught and valued. They serve as an alternative to evolutionary or biological models of inevitable growth.

The Anxiety of Maturation and "Effortless Perfection"

Susan Warner's 1850 novel, *The Wide, Wide World*, tells the story of young Ellen Montgomery, who is pulled from her mother's arms to begin a journey of spiritual development and Christian conversion. Because of her mother's illness and her father's incompetence, Ellen is sent to live with an abrasive aunt. Through a series of trials and with the help of mentors, Ellen learns to be a Christian and is rewarded with love and financial security. The novel went through sixty-seven reprints in the US and was printed in both English and German in Germany.[1] Much has been written about the *The Wide, Wide World* and its influence on Louisa May Alcott's novels and their successors; I focus here on two of Alcott's predecessors and the ways Ellen's experience models important concerns for later Backfisch books.

In 1882, sixteen-year-old Paula Bodewig wrote to Susan Warner from her home in Germany to praise *The Wide, Wide World*. Their brief correspondence of four letters allows us to glimpse one girl's response to Warner's immensely popular novel and reveals several key needs the girls' book will take on directly. Paula labels *The Wide, Wide World* "more than a good companion" and tries to convince Warner to provide individual mentoring. She writes, "I beg you most cordially to answer me, perhaps you understand me better than I myself." Bodewig's plea for mentoring reflects an anxiety about the process of maturing, an anxiety girls' books of the period address. Bodewig wants mentoring; she needs guidance from someone who "understand[s]." Warner's response assumes the solution to Bodewig's uncertainty is a spiritual one—connection with Jesus. She writes, "Only if you have made the right choice, only then you may hope that the Lord Jesus will make himself known to you." Just as Warner's heroine, Ellen Montgomery, can find peace only when she knows herself to be a Christian, Warner believes Bodewig's future happiness and relief from anxiety relies on her Christian conversion.

The question, in this correspondence and in the girls' novels of the same period, is what kind of work will lead a girl to contented womanhood. Bodewig responds, "In fact I am convinced that one will find the truth as well in an anxious, workfilled life as in a tranquil, contemplative way." This is exactly the argument the girls' novel makes. While Ellen Montgomery must retreat to her closet to "find the truth," the heroines of Whitney's and Helm's novels must work in the world to learn to be good women. It is in the labor of sweeping and baking, in the work of demonstrative love, that the girls in these novels are able to convert themselves from girls to women.

Like Paula Bodewig, the readers of *Gretchen's Joys and Sorrows* and *Faith Gartney's Girlhood* experienced uncertainty about how to grow up. This is not just a nineteenth-century problem; in a world where we value "natural" ability over grit, the tools leading to success remain mysterious. For example, in a 2003 study published by the Women's Initiative at Duke University, the committee commented on "a social environment characterized by what one sophomore called 'effortless perfection': the expectation that one would be smart, accomplished, fit, beautiful, and popular, and that all this would happen without visible effort" (Roth 12). In many ways, the work of the Duke study—to make visible the hidden pressures and labor expected of female undergraduates at Duke—is similar to the work of the nineteenth-century women's novel and Backfisch novel. Unlike the Duke study, the Backfisch novel glorifies this system of invisible labor instead of protesting it. But while many twenty-first-century adolescent girls are asked to negotiate a system of invisible labor without instruction or any acknowledgement of the task at hand, the Backfisch book made visible to nineteenth-century girls the work becoming a woman required.

Backfisch novels serve as conduct books that correct the illusion that becoming a woman happens effortlessly. In fact, they explain that performing femininity only appears inevitable because of a deliberate strategy by women to hide the actual labor involved. Successful domestic labor is supposed to be invisible (think of the house elves in the Harry Potter series), and the work of becoming a woman is similarly hidden. Yet for girls like Paula Bodewig, who seek to know themselves and find their place in the world, that work must be described and taught. This then is one function of the Backfisch book, to help its readers understand how to become good women and to accept that work will be required of them. Here the invisible is made visible so the girl reader learns to see the machinery of household work and the effort healthy maturation requires.

Though Ellen, Gretchen, and Faith have different goals set for them, they are aware both of the ways they are lacking and of the models they seek to emulate. And here the three narratives come together. It is clear in all three novels that the protagonist must work to become the kind of woman she and her community want her to be. The work of emotional self-control and self-negation that leads to Ellen's retreat is no longer necessary for Gretchen and Faith. Yet Gretchen and Faith still have work to do to take their places in society. Like Ellen's, their stories make the work of maturation temporarily visible so readers can learn along with them.

Gender as Structure

The models gender theory offers come from the social sciences; this research can be usefully transferred to the realm of the imaginary to help expose the labor the girl's successful transformation requires. I draw here on the work of Barbara Risman and Georgiann Davis, who conceive of gender as "*a social stratification structure* with consequences for individual selves, interactional expectations of others, and embedded in organizations" [italics in original] (1). Their model includes Candace West and Don Zimmerman's concept of "doing gender," which—like the work of Judith Butler—focuses on gender performance as a set of actions that make gender appear normal and ubiquitous.[2] Later research draws out attention to the ways individuals can also "undo gender" in the sense of acting against the expected gendered behaviors of their cultures (Risman and Davis 7).

Critics of the Backfisch book have addressed the ways these books reinforce stereotypical models of femininity. For example, Dagmar Grenz suggests the Backfisch book creates the "illusion . . . that one needs only to live in accordance with social expectations in order to be happy—and especially, in order to be loved" (*Geschichte* 261, my translation). I argue, however, that these books also expose the work of doing gender and provide strategies for "undoing gender."[3]

Gender theory helps us move past an understanding of gender as a series of roles formed by biology or socialization, as Julia McQuillan and I argue in "Why Anne Makes Us Dizzy: Reading *Anne of Green Gables* from a Gender Perspective." Within the novel, gender operates at the individual level, where gender is seen as something characters "have," and at the interactional level, where characters are judged morally in their interactions with others for either reinforcing or transgressing gendered norms and stereotypes. At the institutional level, where genre shapes what can happen in the novel and how readers respond to plot, the novel itself becomes a tool for gender construction.

A theory of gender as structure reminds us that "social structures exist outside individual desires or motives" (Risman and Davis 8) and that individuals and structures have the capacity to influence each other. Joan Acker makes the point in "From Sex Roles to Gendered Institutions" that the term *gendered institutions* illuminates that "gender is present in the processes, practices, images and ideologies, and distributions of power in the various sectors of social life" (567). Risman and Davis are particularly concerned with "the non-reflexive habituated rules, patterns, and beliefs which organize much of human life" and remind us, "Action may turn against structure but can never escape it" (9). This tension between individual action and the constraints of culture and situation is particularly useful for my analysis. It allows us to see that gender is constructed in the Backfisch novel not only through the actions of individuals as they police themselves and each other, but also through gendered plot structures that tie these novels to the earlier sentimental novel and the later adolescent novel.

The next section of this chapter focuses on the structure of the novel as a tool of gender at the institutional level—what Barbara Risman calls, in *Gender Vertigo*, the level of "formal organizational schemas" and "ideological discourse" (29). Risman focuses on the ways ideology shapes social policy; I argue here that the plot arcs that feel satisfactory to us, that create a sense of closure, also rely on gendered ideologies. The chapter then moves to a consideration of gender at the interactional level, in which characters are held "accountable" for the ways in which they "do gender" (West and Zimmerman 136). "Doing gender" creates a "performative link between bodies and gender" and emphasizes accountability, the social policing that works to coerce individuals into appropriate gender display (Risman and Davis 740). In other words, we can think about gender both at the level of plot structure ("what does it mean for the novel to be over?") and in terms of the ways individuals are held accountable to gender stereotypes for their behavior within the novel ("what does it mean to be good?"). Specifically, I will examine the ways domestic labor serves as an example and a metaphor for successful gender performance and plot closure.

Gendered Plot

Immensely popular at the time of publication in the US, *The Wide, Wide World* was also translated and published in Germany and serves as a useful representative of the conversion narrative that is central to the plot of many sentimental novels. Ellen Montgomery is forced to leave a beloved home and connection with her mother, a loss that provokes her to search for a new source of comfort. She is told a relationship with God is the only way to compensate for her sense of loss and learns to put prayer and others first in her life. While she can rely on her mother's love, she will have to earn the love of others, and it is her own behavior that determines whether she will be loved and cared for. Those around her assume Ellen's nature to be sinful; Ellen learns she can only expect to find contentment through suffering, self-control, and, above all, prayer. Ultimately, her efforts pay off with successful spiritual maturation, which leads to her marriage. She is rewarded with a private space of her own and financial resources.

Ellen lives in a world where suffering predominates: her mother is dying, she is placed in the care of unkind individuals, she is constantly reminded that her relationship with God is insufficient, and she suffers heartbreak on a regular basis. In contrast, the Backfisch heroine is surrounded by loving mentors and develops successfully due to her own desire for change. In Clementine Helm's *Gretchen's Joys and Sorrows*, Gretchen leaves her happy home in the country to be educated by her aunt in the city. Through a series of awkward mishaps and embarrassments, she becomes a socially competent woman, is able to help her cousin become more thoughtful, and is rewarded with social success and marriage. Gretchen passes from a loving family home to a loving aunt, is exposed to embarrassment but never real danger, is assured her spirituality is in order, and learns through a series of pleasant (if intimidating) social experiences. The heroine of A. D. T. Whitney's *Faith Gartney's Girlhood* follows a similar trajectory. Faith, the daughter of a well-to-do businessman, encourages her family to move to the country when her father's health and business fail. There, with the help of her aunt, she overcomes errors in judgement and avoids an unfortunate marriage, becomes a useful domestic woman, brings her family back to harmony, and marries a minister. Faith yearns for "some high and holy work of love," learns domestic labor rather than dreams will serve her best, and is surrounded by loving family. On the one hand, we have Ellen, the socially and spiritually vulnerable orphan; on the other, Gretchen and Faith, the pampered and loved society girls. This distinction marks the shift from the sentimental novel for women, with its emotional intensity, to the more playful Backfisch book, in which a happy ending is never far away. It may appear that Ellen's story has little to do with Gretchen's or Faith's.

If we look more carefully at these three novels and the journeys their protagonists take, parallels in both structure and ideology appear. All three novels are organized around a plot structure that moves from loss to learning to transformation to reward. Each novel begins with the girl's realization—through her departure from home and the contrast between her own behavior and that of a role model—that she lacks something (whether a relationship with Jesus, social polish, or self-sufficiency). These novels are thus teleological in that they focus on an outcome and work backward—each girl is presented with a model of the ideal woman and must work to emulate her performance. All three serve as training narratives and take as a central premise the idea that becoming a good woman requires effort and education; all see learning self-control as a central component of that education. In all of these novels, the girl's development is framed as conversion. She goes from being one kind of thing (a sinful child, a Backfisch) to being another kind of thing (a Christian woman, a womanly woman). In all of these cases, successful maturation leads to marriage and the move to a home of her own.

Closure and the Backfisch Book

At the end of *Anne of Green Gables*, when Anne has reconciled herself to focusing on her duty to family rather than to advancing her professional goals, and when the possibilities of a romance plot have been reinforced by her evening walk with Gilbert, the narrator quotes Robert Browning: "God's in His Heaven—/All's right with the world." We can put this book down with a sense of closure and peace because order has been restored. We know at the beginning what the goal in these novels is—a socially adjusted, competent, happy woman. The question is how to get there, and every action along the way is interpreted in terms of whether it moves the protagonist toward or away from that goal. Backfisch heroines do not need to construct a moral code for themselves; they simply need to figure out which authority figures are to be trusted and then take on the moral framework provided by those more expert adults.

In this, the Backfisch novel follows the pattern of the sentimental conversion novel. The desired outcome for a protagonist like Ellen—reflecting the image of God—is clear. The work of the protagonist, then, is to prepare herself for the impression of God's image.[4] Ellen successfully lets go of the self in order to embody her culture's expectations of restrained Christian women; she finds the peace Bodewig so desperately wants for herself. The Backfisch book is linked to *Bildung* (training, shaping) in the sense that it focuses on education and maturation and links closure to happy, productive adulthood.

The Backfisch novel holds on to the sentimental novel's focus on ends and insists on the active participation education requires of the individual. The Backfisch is encouraged to work in a space of self-discovery and is loved before she takes on her culture's images of adult womanhood. In this, the Backfisch novel challenges images of shifting identity as abnormal. Lennard Davis argues eloquently that what makes the novel "new" in the eighteenth century is its link to the new science of the normal. In other words, as Western societies moved from a pyramid version of hierarchy (with God as an unreachable ideal and individuals at various points of closeness or distance from God), to a bell curve (enabled by statistics and the new science of the "average" that relied on the dichotomy of normal/abnormal), "realism" came to mean a focus on the everyday individual in everyday circumstances. Based on this equation of "realistic" with "normal," Davis claims that in early novels, disability (of a main character) is used as a plot device whose resolution simultaneously produces generic resolution of the plot. Davis writes:

> Plot then, in the novel, is really a device to turn what is perceived as the average, ordinary milieu into an abnormal one. Plot functions in the novel, especially during the eighteenth and nineteenth centuries, by temporarily deforming or disabling the fantasy of nation, social class, and gender behaviors that are constructed as norms. The telos of plot aims then to return the protagonists to this norm by the end of the novel.... The end of the novel represents a cure, a repair of the disability, a nostalgic return to a normal time. (330)

Davis suggests one model: that the novel moves from the "normal" to the "abnormal" and back to the "normal," using the protagonist's disability to do so. This lens sees "cure as closure" (330). The Backfisch novel complicates this plot structure because it opens with a protagonist who is one kind of thing—a child—and closes with a protagonist who is another—a woman. What "disables" the girl child is her maturation; behaviors appropriate to her child identity must be defined as immature in order for her to reshape herself. While some novels rely on the physical disabling of the child to effect this change (*What Katy Did*, for example), others rely on the protagonist's own dissatisfaction as she realizes definitions of competence and moral success are tied to age. A good girl is not the same thing as a good woman, and new behaviors will be required of her if she is to maintain her status. West and Zimmerman's notion of "accountability" is useful here as it points to the ways that we act at "*the risk of gender assessment*" (136, italics in original). In the same way men and women are held to different standards within a model of gender accountability, the moral quality of an action is also judged differently when it is performed by a woman rather than a girl. The pressure of gender at the interactional level pushes girls to re-create themselves by reshaping their behavior.

The challenge here is that the labor of womanhood is often invisible. Thus the Backfisch novel fills an important gap for adolescent girls who are aware that their way of being in the world must change if they are to continue to be seen as virtuous. In Davis's terms, the Backfisch book does return to the "norm" of a gendered community, after a period of liminal space in a female-centered world, but the protagonist's role in that community has shifted, because what is normal and appropriate for a girl is unstable and dangerous in a woman.

The Backfisch protagonist is certainly motivated by a desire to be loved—and this psychological need lies behind her journey. The focus of the novel is not her coming to terms with her own psychic place in the world but with her realization that her work maintains the healthy functioning of her community. While the traditional (male) Bildungsroman is about making oneself and one's work visible in the world, the female coming-of-age novel is about making one's work invisible and achieving "effortless perfection." The Backfisch book both participates in that pattern and acknowledges it.

By watching Ellen learn to retire to her closet to keep her spiritual life in order, the work of becoming a Christian becomes apparent to readers. By watching as Faith learns to run a household, readers learn the secret strategies of successful womanhood. These books serve as conduct manuals in the ways they lay out clear goals for contemporary readers and instructions for achieving those goals.

From the Spiritual to the Domestic

The central problem of the sentimental novel *The Wide, Wide World* is established early: Ellen loves her mother more than she loves Jesus. The project of this novel is to move Ellen to a space where her discomfort and sense of misery are so intense that she is forced to turn to God. Her mother goes so far as to tell Ellen: "If losing your mother might be the means of finding you that better Friend,

I should be quite willing and glad to go for ever." In her immaturity, Ellen's response is to sob. But by the end of the novel Ellen will have embraced this principle and agreed that her salvation is more important than her emotional comfort. In contrast, the Backfisch Gretchen already has her spiritual life in order; in fact, it serves as a model for her domestic work. In the Backfisch novel, Christianity is taken as a given; unlike *The Wide, Wide World*, in *Gretchen's Joys and Sorrows*, a relationship with God is a source of comfort and security, not something to be worked for. Ellen's intense anxiety about her spiritual life and salvation is replaced, in the Backfisch novel, by a fear of social embarrassment and a desire for social competence.

Ellen's spiritual uncertainty is accompanied by a model of relationships that says she is responsible for making others love her. On the eve of leaving for her Aunt Fortune's house, Ellen worries that she will be unloved. Mrs. Montgomery responds:

> Her loving or not loving you will depend solely and entirely upon yourself, Ellen. Don't forget that. If you are a good child, and make it your daily care to do your duty, she cannot help liking you, be she what she may; and on the other hand, if she have all the will in the world to love you, she cannot do it unless you will let her,—it all depends on your behaviour.

In fact, Aunt Fortune is not particularly fond of Ellen, and according to Mrs. Montgomery's theory, Ellen's behavior has failed completely. Throughout this novel, Ellen not only suffers, but is told her suffering is her own responsibility and a mark of her own failure (to love God and please others).

While Gretchen experiences homesickness at leaving her family, her parting carries with it no sense of tragedy; we are all confident she will return safely to her parents and siblings. Her aunt is a source of comfort, rather than a trial, and when Gretchen mourns the parting from her family, Aunt Ulrike "softly stroked my hand . . . and spoke so tenderly to me that I soon became calm" (1). Gretchen has yet to do anything to earn her aunt's love; like her relationship with God, it appears to be her right rather than something to be earned.

On her first night in a strange house, Gretchen is overwhelmed with homesickness, until she remembers to ask God for help. She tells us: "But at last I quietly folded my hands, and sought peace and comfort of Him who, even here, watched over me, and upon whose kind, fatherly protection and guidance I could now, as ever, rely" (5). Mrs. Montgomery would be proud; it seems Gretchen begins her journey where Ellen ends up.

While the story of Faith Gartney—protagonist of a second Backfisch book, *Faith Gartney's Girlhood*—begins with her desire to "rouse to some high and holy work of love" (17), both she and Gretchen quickly learn the path to greatness begins with less exalted language. Faith's aunt tells her, "Just take hold of the first thing that comes in your way. If the Lord's got anything bigger to give you, he'll see to it. There's your mother's mending-basket brimful of stockings" (220). Similarly, when Gretchen's cousin Eugenie is appalled Gretchen is doing what she considers the servant's work of mending stockings, Gretchen tells her she "did not know that such work was dishonorable." She explains, "Auntie says the less help we need from others, the better off we are, because we make ourselves so much the more independent of other men" (50). While Ellen Montgomery must learn to be independent by developing a close relationship with Jesus, Faith's and Gretchen's independence is of a more practical nature. We never see Faith or Gretchen in church; we do see them become increasingly skilled as housekeepers.

Thus the sentimental novel and Backfisch story require distinct forms of work from their heroines. As Jane Tompkins writes:

> For what the word *sentimental* really means in this context is that the arena of human action, as in the Tract Society directions, has been defined not as the world, but as the human soul. This fiction shares with the evangelical reform movement a theory of power that stipulates that all true action is not material, but spiritual; that one obtains spiritual power through prayer; and that those who know how, in the privacy of their closets, to struggle for possession of their souls will one day possess the world through the power given to them by God. (151)

In *The Wide, Wide World*, Ellen Montgomery needs to learn to be quiet. Her explosive sobbing and back talk are depicted as markers of childishness; when she gains maturity, she learns to retreat to her closet and her room at the top of the house. Ellen's spiritual maturity is marked by the way she occupies physical space. She learns self-control by removing herself from public spaces and shutting up her exuberant despair behind closed doors. The project for the Backfisch heroine is somewhat different. She too must learn to hide, but her discretion plays out in plain sight. The good woman is primarily a social woman, in the girls' book, and her job is to look peaceful and at ease even when she is engaged in intense physical and emotional labor.

In Backfisch books, material action allows for spiritual action. A character achieves spiritual power by tidying and dusting, by setting her person and home to rights. She succeeds by creating social situations in which her effort is invisible. Her power comes not from retreating to the closet, but by hosting parties in which the social fabric of the community is reinforced. Only her mentor and the reader see the work that lies behind effortless perfection.

While Ellen's journey takes her away from the ideal mother figure who serves as a role model and loves her unconditionally, Gretchen's journey takes her from a loving mother to a loving mother figure. Ellen's goal is to be just like her mother; Gretchen's is to improve on her mother, not in her loving nature, but in terms of her education. In both cases, these girls (and their readers) know early what is expected of them. Mrs. Montgomery tells Ellen: "You know fully what I wish you to do and to be," and Ellen agrees—she is to learn to love Jesus as her mother does and to practice self-control, which means mirroring her mother's behavior (14). Women in this novel—from Ellen's mother, to her aunt Fortune, to her mentor Alice—define Ellen's outbursts and her resentment against those she feels treat her unfairly and her emotional outbursts as sins against her mother and God; it is when she "behave[s] beautifully" that she is praised (9). Mrs. Montgomery's isolation—though ostensibly the result of her illness—also becomes a model for Ellen. Over the course of the novel Ellen learns to retire to her closet or room to pray; by the end of the novel, she has been rewarded with an inner room. Ellen's goal is not just to manage her emotions in such a way that they are not obvious to others, but to literally withdraw to an interior physical space.

Gretchen's challenge is a different one; she needs to learn social graces, and Aunt Ulrike is a perfect role model: "There was something in my aunt's character that excited my secret admiration, and yet there was nothing at all striking in her manner; on the contrary, all appeared so simple, so natural, that it seemed as if one must always so speak and act" (1). It turns out this apparently "natural" behavior is the result of significant knowledge and labor. As Gretchen learns on her first morning in Berlin, when the work of preparing her body for the day takes up the whole of a chapter, presenting a "natural" body to the world involves careful scrubbing and braiding and a vast quantity of soap. Aunt Ulrike tells Gretchen, "The advancement of a country is indicated by its consumption of soap; the more used, the greater the progress" (6). The work of washing her body is the first step in Gretchen's study of how to control it.

Her education continues as she is "inwardly planed and polished" through an education in languages, music, and drawing.[5] There is no mention of religious education (though the American translation interprets *innerlich* as "spiritually" rather than "inwardly," giving the work a religious connotation). Gretchen is defined as a good child by everyone around her. Her project is to learn to be a good woman, which doesn't mean any shift in character/inner self, but simply in how she presents that self to the world. Her errors are not sins, but "mistakes in etiquette," and the label of Backfisch gives her a free space in which to make those mistakes. Her aunt's role is to be sure her intrinsically good nature is appropriately nurtured. As Aunt Ulrike tells Gretchen: "Who sits crooked, grows crooked. The tree that as a feeble stem is trained straight, is a magnificent stately tree in age" (22). It is Aunt Ulrike's task to provide that training, which must strike a delicate balance between preserving Gretchen's "childlike naturalness" and training her to be "cultured." The danger here is that a girl's education will lead to pretension and egotism and undo her innocent nature. Here Aunt Ulrike sounds much like the grandmother in Alcott's *An Old-Fashioned Girl* in her distinction between society women who draw attention to their performance of femininity and good women who appear to have developed naturally.

As Faith and Gretchen develop into capable housekeepers, they are also taught that the effective performance of domesticity (and femininity) requires an illusion of effortlessness. Gretchen tells her reader, "Above all, auntie wished me to do all quietly, so that the guests might not notice the motion of the machinery by which the work was carried out." She repeats her aunt's lesson that

> I always feel very uncomfortable when in visiting I see the trouble that my presence sometimes occasions. There are [*sic*] running and calling, doors and closets opened and shut, hurrying to and fro, clicking, blustering and knocking about, perhaps only to get me a piece of cake or serve tea. Never make a noise about anything dear daughter, either in spiritual or worldly matters. (21)

The "machinery" of Gretchen's work is domestic rather than industrial—but Gretchen is to teach herself to operate as an unseen machine, consistent, efficient, and silent. She is to make it appear that the work of grooming herself and running a household is effortless. Her work is done best when others can ignore it. Gretchen's education encompasses not only the details of care of her person, guests in her home, and the business of making calls on friends, but also the need to keep silent the "creaking of the wheels" that the running of a household requires. In order for guests to feel comfortable, the work their presence requires must be invisible; in order to teach the girl how to perform that labor, it must be made temporarily visible. Through domestic labor, the invisible work of gender performance is also made visible. Girl readers learn through anecdotes that balance the girl's natural sweetness with her need for education that becoming a woman requires work rather than simply waiting for maturity.

This quotation also brings us to my next point: the link between the domestic and the spiritual, which functions somewhat differently for the German Gretchen and the American Faith. Aunt Ulrike tells Gretchen:

> Every evening, before you go to bed, examine carefully all the clothing that you intend to wear the next day, and put everything in order. One has always sufficient time for that, and if a little sleep is lost thereby it does not matter much. As one examines his heart and soul before sleeping, and resolves to correct what has been wrong during the day, so should he also put the outer man in order. One should always bear in mind that such little habits bear good fruits, while little neglects soon grow to be large ones, so well in dress as in the heart, and then every reparation requires ten-fold care and labor. (7)

The assumption here is that Gretchen's spiritual life, unlike Ellen's, is already in order and can serve as a model for her physical self-presentation. By preparing herself for the next day before bed—when the time spent will merely result in a private loss of sleep—Gretchen can show the world a neat appearance that seems natural.

In *Faith Gartney's Girlhood*, the link between the domestic and spiritual is framed somewhat differently, but relies on the same idea that domestic labor should be the primary concern of a girl's life. After Faith has moved to the country and taken over care of the household, the narrator tells us:

> It was a bright, happy face that glanced hither and thither, about the house, those fair summer mornings; and it wasn't the hands alone that were busy, as under their dexterous and delicate touch all things arranged themselves in attractive and graceful order, thought straightened and cleared itself, as furniture and books were dusted and set right; and while the carpet brightened under the broom, something else brightened and strengthened, also, within.

This passage suggests that only by doing the physical labor life sets in front of her can Faith hope to become a good woman; it is in her usefulness that she proves herself and develops spiritually. The move between active and passive voice in this passage both reveals and hides Faith's work. The things "arranged themselves" and thought "cleared itself," but it is Faith who dusts and sets right. Gretchen's Aunt Ulrike would be proud as Faith carries out the daily tasks of housekeeping cheerfully and without apparent effort.

The Work of Performing Gender

Both kinds of texts examined in this chapter—sentimental novels for women and girls' stories—rely on work as a central principle. Instead of focusing on their protagonists' spiritual development, the Backfisch book makes visible two kinds of work—the machinery of running a household and the personal work of developing a mature (social) identity. By highlighting the hard work needed to turn a girl into a woman, these novels show that becoming a woman is not a natural, inevitable process, but a form of transformation that occurs in a social context and requires mentorship, trial and error, and perseverance. The mundane nature of domestic labor stands in contrast to the mystery of evolution and the curious conversion of an active, heedless girl into a womanly woman.

Backfisch novels also claim that the complexities of growing up, which lead to the anxiety surrounding maturation Bodewig describes, can be simplified and organized through the mechanism of teaching successful domesticity. A domestic metaphor is useful here: in *Gretchen's Joys and Sorrows*, Eugenie memorizes recipes to please her fiancé; she also experiments with cooking and baking. The ambiguous nature of the girl's transformation is made visible in two ways: first, by providing a recipe for success in the story of a girl's transformation, which includes the details of approved behavior; and second, by providing a clear model of the desired outcome. Baking a cake is an encouraging metaphor because it models explicit directions and an easily evaluated outcome. The mystery of the chemical action of baking powder and eggs is made reassuringly comprehensible in the clarity of a recipe and in a measurable goal—either the cake rose or it didn't. The Backfisch novel suggests that if you can learn to bake a cake, you can learn to be a good woman; while both projects require diligence, the model of fictional heroines is an antidote to the anxiety surrounding maturation. As Risman and Davis point out, citing Berk (1985): "Households have become 'gender factories' where women do more of the labor because by doing so, they are doing gender itself" (7). The Backfisch novel draws our attention to that work and in so doing, I argue, makes visible both domestic labor and the labor of making a woman out of an adolescent girl.

These books do not primarily explore the individual's experience; instead, they judge that experience in terms of whether it leads to a happy, moral life or not. In the same way we judge the success of a cake by the product that gets brought to the table, the Backfisch novel evaluates the protagonist's journey in terms of the desired outcome, not the process. These novels can be read as cookbooks providing instruction, where each step is linked to a final goal. Like a cookbook, the Backfisch novel demystifies the magic of transforming ingredients into a dish greater than the sum of its parts. Eugenie uses cooking as an ongoing tool for expressing her joking temperament—she serves a sand cake for tea, for example—but her successful maturation is signified by the fact that she learns to produce delicious food. We focus not on her internal narrative (the novel is never focalized through Eugenie), but on her actions; we judge those actions based on their results, not her intentions.

While neither domestic labor nor doing gender are instinctive actions, both are supposed to be performed without fuss. There is a comfort in being taught how to do things right—in the making explicit a hidden agenda with significant moral consequences. While the conversion narrative provides step-by-step instruction in the process of transforming yourself spiritually, the Backfisch book provides a similar set of instructions for secular, gendered success. When Ellen Montgomery is led weeping to begin the journey toward her own salvation, she establishes a model of the female Bildungsroman that outlives the genre of sentimental fiction itself. While later novels shift to more secular concerns, the pattern established in the conversion narrative continues to structure girls' fiction. If we read these books as conversion narratives, they reveal several key ideas about the acquisition of gender.

First, Backfisch books force us to acknowledge that becoming a "womanly woman" is hard work and requires ongoing effort. (Backfisch heroines are neither able to maintain a childhood freedom from feminine roles nor are they able to move effortlessly into these roles.) We can usefully consider the labor required of girls and women in the context of the work of "doing gender."[6]

Second, these texts make a link between conversion (to Christianity or womanhood) and virtue. Becoming a womanly woman may even replace Christian salvation as the moral goal of a woman's life. Learning to maintain a household and family is one aspect of learning to perform femininity. It shares with gender acquisition a moral imperative—domestic labor is one thing good women do well—but includes visible and concrete definitions of success.

Third, these texts must come to terms with the paradox that while the successful woman doesn't display either her salvation or her domestic labor, somehow girls must learn to perform the invisible labor necessary for "virtuous" womanhood. The advantage of domestic work is that it can be taught and success is clear—this makes the ambiguous process of becoming a woman something that can be defined, learned, and documented.

Backfisch books insist that while the physical development into womanhood may be inevitable, the psychological absorption of "womanly" virtue requires hard work, must be deliberately chosen, and is the prerequisite to real happiness and power for women. They portray femininity itself as a conversion experience that follows a similar pattern to religious conversion and that holds similar possibilities for failure. Just as, according to Warner, the truths of the Bible are most powerful when associated with the pleasures of youth, so too is gender best learned early and through the delights of reading. Ellen Montgomery's story assumes her femininity and details her conversion to Christianity. Novels for girls assume a Christian identity and focus on the successful performance of femininity. If we read girls' books as conversion narratives, they help us to acknowledge becoming a "useful woman" is hard work and requires ongoing individual efforts rather than a smooth inevitable progression. They also highlight the transference of moral judgment from spiritual development to gendered development. Becoming a useful woman rather than a good Christian becomes the central goal of a girl's education; if she mends enough stockings, her salvation will take care of itself.

On the surface, Backfisch books appear quite distinct from the adolescent fiction that would appear a hundred years later. Their protagonists live in protected, white, middle- or upper-class worlds; they do not question whether they will be fed or loved; and their stories avoid any direct reference to sex or abuse. The instructive tone of these novels also appears to distinguish them from contemporary adolescent literature. Even when written in the first person, the narrator is an adult who looks back on her past, rather than a teenager writing about her present. And yet these books draw our attention to a realism often ignored even in contemporary adolescent literature—the work of feeding a family, cleaning a household, and educating the next generation. The Backfisch book is in the confusing situation of making domestic and social work visible in order to hide it again in a return to a fairy-tale narrative of happy ever after. What the reader has learned about the work required to maintain that fairy tale—the shoveling of ashes and kneading of bread—is not unlearned simply because that work again retreats into the background. What further distinguishes these novels from some later adolescent novels is the role of adults. Although the Backfisch has domestic and emotional labor to do, and things to learn about the world, she does so not in opposition to the adults around her, but with their support.

By tracing the ways the plot of the Backfisch novel relies on an evangelical model of conversion drawn from the sentimental novel, we see more clearly that these novels envision the acquisition of gendered womanhood as hard work. Becoming a woman is not natural or inevitable; it requires training, perseverance, and practice. As twenty-first-century readers, we may well deplore the ways Gretchen and Faith are taught that the path to a happy life is through domesticity and self-control. There is a narrowness of possibility for girls in these novels and a moral didacticism that links pleasing others with virtue. And yet Gretchen and Faith are allowed to doubt themselves, to feel deeply, to have mood swings, and still be told they are understood, that their experience is normal. In the twenty-first century, we have shifted from seeing domestic work as the solution to the uncomfortable reality of being human to defining lability as mental illness. A 2019 editorial in *Lancet Psychiatry* argues, for example, that "borderline personality disorder is not so much a diagnosis as it is a liminal state" and a contemporary discomfort with emotional intensity and shifting identities may well be one reason so many adolescent girls in America struggle with depression ("Beyond the Borderline").

The Backfisch novel certainly does work to curb the girl's strong and variable emotions. There is the instruction Gretchen gets from her friend Marie, for example, about hiding her emotions behind a public face. The difference between what Gretchen is taught and what we expect of today's girls is that while for Gretchen, the public self is to be contained and controlled, there is an acknowledgement of a private self that feels deeply, that changes moment to moment. When we seek to control girls through psychiatric drugs rather than domestic work, we move to a model that insists on regulating the private space as well as the public one, to creating not just the appearance of stable femininity, but also the inner experience of content detachment.

The Backfisch novel helps us imagine another view of adolescence, one where emotional lability and a sense of uncertainty result not in alienation and a diagnosis of mental disease, but in community support and acceptance. It thus provides alternatives to both the model of Christian conversion—allowing the self to be remade by God—and to contemporary psychiatric models—allowing the self to be remade by modern medicine. The Backfisch book imagines adolescence as hard work, where the nurture of loving adults and peers and explicit instruction on how to contribute to domestic life provides a balance to the normal variation of human identity. It suggests baking cakes and mending stockings are viable alternatives to both prayer and pills.

· CHAPTER FOUR ·
The Backfisch and Fantasies of Growth

> Men and women grew fast in those days of the nation's trouble and danger, and Jane awoke from the vague dull dream she had hitherto called life to new hopes, new fears, new purposes. Then after a year's anxiety, a year when one never looked in the newspaper without dread and sickness of suspense, came the telegram saying that Tom was wounded; and without so much as asking Miranda's leave, she packed her trunk and started for the South. She was in time to hold Tom's hand through hours of pain; to show him for once the heart of a prim New England girl when it is ablaze with love and grief; to put her arms about him so that he could have a home to die in, and that was all—all, but it served.
>
> (REBECCA OF SUNNYBROOK FARM, CHAPTER 3)

In chapter 3 of Kate Douglas Wiggin's 1903 novel *Rebecca of Sunnybrook Farm*, the mystery of the contrast between Rebecca's two aunts—Miranda's pinched lips and Jane's loving heart—is explained in terms of the past. Jane's experience of anxiety and suffering, her chance to love and sacrifice, "served" to help her mature emotionally and prepared her to mother her young niece in a way her sister Miranda could not. The explicit link between Jane's maturation and the United States Civil War that is made in this early twentieth-century novel is part of a larger pattern in the girls' book; this chapter explores that pattern.

Many scholars have analyzed the ways that nineteenth-century children's literature contributed to fictions of nationalism. The girls' novel is one place where the significance of women and girls to the reproduction of fictions of nationalism appears in the nineteenth century. If we focus on the girl herself, the Backfisch novel reinforces gendered notions of the girl's limited (but significant) impact on her community and nation. If we look instead at the structure of the Backfisch novel, the narrative arc that moves from innocence, to loss, to pain, to maturity emerges as a model for successful nation-building. Perhaps novels about adolescent girls became best sellers in the second half of the nineteenth century in Germany and the United States rather than in other Western countries because both countries were engaged in a process of unification rather than expansion.

Unlike older European countries, for which the nineteenth century was an age of colonialism, the United States and Germany "were focused inward, developing—intentionally or not—the centralizing powers that have defined the modern state ever since," as historian Kenneth Weisbrode argues in his essay "Why Bismarck Loved Lincoln." This inward focus becomes a literary as well as political theme. David Ehrenpreis points out that "the term Bildungsroman entered general usage at about the same time that Germany achieved political unification" (10) and "beginning around 1870, German scholars began to view the maturation of the hero in the Bildungsroman as a parable for the development of the German nation toward cultural independence and political unification" (xiii). Ehrenpreis asks what it is women writers contribute to this parable and why they have been ignored. The Backfisch book, with its focus on interior work and commitment to community identity, models a different kind of coming-of-age, one that also resonates with the creation of national identity.

Woman-building and nation-building both craft identities by shaping disparate realities into a common fantasy. The Backfisch novel allows us to imagine adolescent transformation and the celebration of social maturity, while "the nation" pushes soldiers and civilians to engage in great wars. The fantasy of nation—the "imagined political community," in Benedict Anderson's term—carries such psychological power that individuals will give their lives to create and perpetuate it (5). In this chapter, I unpack the connections between woman-building and nation-building by reading two Backfisch novels—the American *What Katy Did*, by Susan Coolidge (1872); the German *Das Heideprinzesschen*, by Eugenie Marlitt (1871), translated into English in 1872 under the title *The Little Moorland Princess*; Otto von Bismarck's "Blut und Eisen" ("Blood and Iron") speech (1862); and Abraham Lincoln's Gettysburg Address (1863). While Bismarck and Lincoln go about defining borders in different ways (for Bismarck the nation is about Prussian power; for Lincoln the nation is about liberty), they both appeal to national identity and unity, call for sacrifice, and assert that pain can spur growth. Books for adolescent girls reflect, reinforce, and trouble key themes the US and Germany explored as they attempted to move their states from "adolescence" to mature power and function. By imagining the adolescent girl's contributions not only as the work she does, but also as her ability to transform herself models productive growth, the Backfisch book helps us reenvision adolescence.

The Girl as Part of the "Great Social Household"

Girls' books contribute to a gendered project in which children are trained in national values; girls learn that domestic labor allows them to participate in and sustain what German historians call the "great social household." This image links domestic life with political life and imagines the work women do in the home as of national significance; the nation is an expanded family and every citizen has a role to play. Ann Taylor Allen points to the fact that for German feminists, "in women's political discourse, 'motherhood' became a metaphorical term for a distinctly female claim to rights based on women's service to society" (11). Similarly, as Mary P. Ryan suggests, in the US the term "the mother's empire" reflects the belief that the home was "the imperial center, the mother country, from which women launched their vast social influence" (145).

Jennifer Drake Askey's book, *Good Girls, Good Germans*, describes the ways authors of educational and fictional texts for girls "saw the domestic activities of young, middle-class women as constituting their national involvement" (172). Askey argues these texts "participated in the creation of a vision—and an experience—of girlhood in Germany that drew girls and women actively into the national community" (10); Anne Scott MacLeod further argues that "it was believed that the youngest members of the new political system must be taught that upholding this system was morally sanctioned" (88). In *Mädchenliteratur der Kaiserzeit* (Girls' Literature of the Imperial Empire), Gisela Wilkending argues that one function of the girls' book is to spread "German-ness" in the same way nonfiction texts link girls to political and cultural memory. The link between the girl's story and her nation is determined by the gendered work that she does, and girls' fiction contributes to the education of girls who will replicate national ideals in their labor and in their political beliefs.

If we focus on the girl in terms of the contributions she makes as an individual worker, the power girls could access came from a mechanistic model that saw every part as essential to the workings of the whole. In chapter 3 of Susan Coolidge's *What Katy Did*, Katy's father shows this mindset by repeating the "old saying":

> For the want of a nail the shoe was lost,
> For the want of a shoe the horse was lost,
> For the want of a rider the battle was lost,
> For the want of a battle the kingdom was lost,
> And all for the want of a horse-shoe nail.

Katy replies, "Who would have thought such a little speck of a thing as not sewing on my string could make a difference?" Katy is herself "a little speck of a thing," but she learns in the course of this novel that her behavior has a huge impact on her family. Backfisch literature suggests girls are the "nails" that keep the kingdom together.

The work they do may seem insignificant, but without it the whole nation falls. While sewing on strings is one of Katy's least favorite tasks (close, in fact, to her dislike for mending stockings), this novel suggests she needs to reimagine that work as one of familial and national significance in order to see herself as part of the machine of the modern world.

Dr. Carr's lesson echoes that of Aunt Ulrike in *Gretchen's Joys and Sorrows*. Aunt Ulrike tells Gretchen, "Who accustoms himself to consider others in little things, will not be unmindful of his fellow-creatures in large ones" (61), a remark we might see as justifying the Backfisch heroine's domestic education. By learning to pay attention to details—household details, the feelings of those around them, the needs of the poor—the girl will allow society to function smoothly. When contemporary German critics referred to Backfisch literature as "Trivialliterature" as a slur, they were neglecting the significance of the trivial and the fact that nations are built on the apparently insignificant. Without a new generation of "useful women," what would happen to Germany? To the US?

The answer comes in part in the distinction made between Gretchen's mother, whose loving care marks her as a virtuous woman, and her cousin Eugenie's mother, whom Eugenie comes to realize is "worthless" in comparison with Gretchen's (62). Eugenie's unkindnesses and vanity are positioned as the fault of her unfit mother. According to the Backfisch novel, girls will not inevitably become good women; when they don't, either other women (like Aunt Ulrike) can try to fix the vain, flippant daughters they raise, or the pattern of self-centered womanhood will be repeated in another generation. In the latter case, another generation of men will be left without the comfort and stability of a happy home. The girl is part of the great social household not only because she contributes to the successful functioning of society, but also because when she is properly trained, she allows for men to imagine their own happy futures.

By the end of *Gretchen's Joys and Sorrows*, for example, the "family" of women this narrative describes no longer exists: Eugenie has married the Baron, Gretchen has married the doctor, Marie has found a minister husband, and Aunt Ulrike has gone off to keep house for her brother-in-law. A community of women comes together for a brief period so that four happy households can be created. Order is restored in the form of heterosexual pairings at the end of this novel, showing how the stability of the nation depends on the work women do in the home and in training each other.

The "great social household" gives individuals the illusion of power while still maintaining patriarchal systems. David Ehrenpreis describes the success of Eugenie Marlitt's fiction in Germany as "a careful balancing act" that worked by "encouraging the hopes and flattering the desires of the subjugated, while remaining unthreatening to those in control" (185). Joe Sutliff Sanders makes a similar point about American sentimental fiction, which he describes as "power fantasies for an oppressed cultural minority and an endorsement of the status quo all at once" (185). Growing nations require that girls grow up in a particular way, and these novels provide a model of how girls can contribute to emotional nationalism and to the work of the households upon which the nation rests.

If we see girls only in terms of their contributions to the household (and thus to the nation), they appear to lose individuality and power as they develop. As Joe Sutliff Sanders says of orphan girl novels in *Disciplining Girls*, "These are narratives about the restoration of a temporarily derailed patriarchy and the character types that support it, not about the first construction of genuine, empowered individuals" (47). Like the orphan girl heroines Sanders describes, Backfisch heroines begin as individuals—at odds with their communities—and learn to support community identity and become part of the "great social household." This trajectory makes them happy, content, and peaceful, whereas being an individual made them feel awkward, angry, ill, and uncomfortable. These girls start to see themselves in terms of their relationship to their communities rather than focusing on themselves. They thus model the ideal citizen in a system that works seamlessly, the citizen whose sense of their identity is always negotiated in terms of an imagined nation and its needs.

The individual process of maturation described in the girls' novel also complements the collective experience. In the rest of this chapter I move beyond the idea of the girl as a "nail" to argue that narratives of adolescent development provide another point of entry into nineteenth-century anxieties about national growth. The girl herself may give up her individual will to accommodate the national good, but her story continues to reinforce adolescence as a space of powerful transformation.

Narratives of Adolescence

Backfisch novels reflect and make apparent key elements of the project of nation-building, rather than simply serving as a window into contemporary ideas about girls and their journey toward womanhood. These novels assure girls their contributions to the nation are essential and powerful. They also address cultural concerns: how does a community create order out of chaos? How do we build unified nations out of pain? Both the US and Germany are looking for narratives that support fantasies of national unity. The success of the Backfisch novel may result not only from its appeal to the fantasies of adolescent girls (as Askey describes), but also because it provides reassurance to a wider community.

Political speeches shaped national discourse in the nineteenth century: Bismarck's "Blood and Iron" speech is seen as shifting the German states toward a united empire, and the Gettysburg Address is widely recognized as shaping the imagined American nation that became a world power. Similarly, narratives for girls not only described how girls contributed to the nation but also suggested the journey of the adolescent girl could serve as a valuable model for the national journey toward wholeness and power.

On September 30, 1862, Otto von Bismarck came before the budget commission of the Prussian Parliament as the newly appointed minister of Prussia. The commission was reluctant to approve military spending, but Bismarck argued the time for negotiation was past and the future of Prussia required the willingness to fight and to spend. Bismarck argued Prussia should be powerful rather than liberal—should assert itself with military force rather than debate the merits of constitutional authority—because, as he claims in the most famous phrase of his "Blood and Iron" speech, "it is not by speeches and majority resolutions that the great questions of the time are decided . . . but by iron and blood." Unlike the French, whom Bismarck saw as willing to sacrifice power for community agreement, Bismarck defines the Prussians as an independent people who require military preparedness to form a healthy, vital state. Over the next eight years, Bismarck would win three wars against neighboring countries, shape the new German empire, and become its first chancellor. His success reinforced the ideals of German independence, power, and willingness to sacrifice both money and blood. While these wars are often referred to as the wars of German unification, they were simultaneously wars of exclusion. In the interests of protecting the powers of the Prussians, for example, Austria was excluded from the German empire.

Eugenie Marlitt's *Das Heideprinzesschen* (*The Little Moorland Princess*), published nine years after this speech and in the immediate wake of unification, addresses questions of borders and privilege, pain as a necessary price for power, and the privileging of economic power over idealism—issues implicit in Bismarck's speech. This first-person narrative moves us from Lenore's childhood home on the moors, where she grows up "untrained and merry-hearted, like the willows by the stream" (34), to the recognition that she "knows nothing and understands nothing" (77), to her education in the city. As I discuss in chapter 1, Lenore's interactions first with her father, and then with her future husband, awaken "that feminine instinct within the wild, wanton child" (102). Without the support of othermothers, Lenore is left more vulnerable than other Backfisch heroines, but her success is similarly marked by her realization that she must move from wildness to civilization, and that domestic experience will help her do so. Lenore herself must choose what to acknowledge as "self" and what to exclude. She learns the rewards of a painful education and learns to celebrate the mercantile class over the aristocracy. Her successful growth, from an uncultivated wild child to a socially and financially competent woman, and the sacrifices this growth requires of her, link her story to fantasies of nation-building.

In November of 1863, Abraham Lincoln gave the Gettysburg Address, a call to redefine the nation "conceived" in 1776 and now engaged in a period of "testing." He asked for "the living . . . to be dedicated . . . to the unfinished work" of those who died at Gettysburg and called on his audience to "take increased devotion to that cause . . . that this nation, under God, shall have a new birth of freedom—and that government of the people, by the people, for the people, shall not perish from the earth." There are three key elements of this speech for my purposes: the idea of a united "people" with a sense of solidarity and community, the need to make the sacrifice and pain of war meaningful, and the positioning of the United States as a nation in need of rebirth.

Susan Coolidge's *What Katy Did* allows us to examine these issues from a very different narrative perspective. Katy crosses borders, goes to "The School of Pain," and tempers her natural exuberance with mature self-control. Katy must acknowledge her carelessness and its costs and be willing to suffer for her own good and that of her community to take on a successful mature identity. In her story, pain becomes a tool of maturation rather than an evil to be avoided. While this novel is explicitly a fantasy of a girl finding purpose and love, it implicitly reinforces a narrative of national growth through pain toward community and responsibility.

Through stories of adolescent transformation, these novels show how something awkward, painful, and uncomfortable can resolve into connection and self-assurance. They also show how the natural can be preserved in the civilized: for the girl, natural girlish charm is still present in the womanly identity that provides social power; for the nation, the idea of a natural, tribal identity is preserved in the state that provides political power.

Making Meaning out of Suffering

The American *What Katy Did* and the German *The Little Moorland Princess* emerged at a time when both the United States and Germany were working to define mature national identities. Bismarck's

"Blood and Iron" speech serves to ignite a willingness to fight and sacrifice; writing before the wars of German unification, he proposes the German nation must be willing to pay with blood for national identity. Speaking in the midst of the United States Civil War, Lincoln works to redefine loss of life as a meaningful sacrifice in the service of the ideal of democracy. While the values that lay behind each leader's actions may have been quite different—as Michael Beran argues, Bismarck was motivated by expediency, Lincoln by moral imagination—both worked to convince their people that suffering was a mark of success rather than loss, an act of progress rather than a sign of failure. Similarly, *What Katy Did* casts pain as a form of education, a school where God is teacher. *The Little Moorland Princess* justifies the pain of education as a means to a better, more mature end. Physical, emotional, and intellectual pain act as a kind of crucible for the girl protagonists, refining what is best in them and burning away the insensitivity and awkwardness of youth. We can see parallels between this productive pain and the pain necessary to Lincoln's "nation, under God" and Bismarck's "healthy, vital state." Katy and Lenore are better for their pain, and so perhaps could be the United States and Germany.

The Backfisch heroine acts on a domestic stage rather than a national one, but her story similarly engages with the discomfort of change. For these books' heroines, suffering is progressive rather than tragic. They thus provide an alternative to Robin Bernstein's compelling argument that childhood functions as "an act of surrogation that compensates for losses incurred through growth" (205). Katy and Lenore are empowered adolescents, not vulnerable children. They play a different literary role from that of the "suffering child"—the child, in Anna Mae Duane's perspective, whose "symbolic role in mediating cultural and colonial violence shaped the definition of childhood itself as a site of vulnerability, suffering, and victimhood" (3). When Katy endures physical pain and Lenore experiences emotional upheaval, their suffering pushes them toward self-transformation. While the romantic child relies on a pastoral, natural past, the agential adolescent points to a productive, exciting future.

The Backfisch book makes explicit the education that shapes a girl into a good woman. By making this work visible in one character, it makes wider claims that apply to human subjects more generally, and even to nations. The Backfisch book sets aside the suffering child in favor of the adolescent girl whose story models successful growth. If we romanticize the past—by holding on to nostalgic visions of childhood or prewar community identities—the pain of growth may not seem worthwhile. If we focus on a successful future, pain becomes an uncomfortable but profitable evil. The Backfisch book reimagines childhood suffering as adolescent growing pains, and its readers might have seen the pain of war, like the pain of adolescence, as necessary to change and maturity.

The pain of adolescence refashions the girl into a new kind of person, in the same way the suffering of war reforms the United States and Germany into new kinds of countries. There's a mystery in this, the telos that turns acorns into oak trees. The potential Lincoln saw for the future of the United States, or Bismarck saw for the German empire, existed already—the question was what kind of effort, education, and rhetoric would bring forth that new nation. This is a question with which the nineteenth-century novel for girls was already engaged—how to call forth a womanly woman from the chaos, untidiness, and emotional intensity of adolescence.

Katy's first response to her accident—a fall from a swing that results from "the want of the small 'horseshoe nail' of Obedience"—is resentment and despair. Her Aunt Helen reframes her misfortune as an educational opportunity. She says in chapter 9, "Now, Katy Carr, you wanted to go to school and learn to be wise and useful, and here's a chance for you. God is going to let you go to *His* school—where He teaches all sorts of beautiful things to people." She continues, "It is called the School of Pain . . . The rules of the school are pretty hard, but the good scholars, who keep them best, find out after a while how right and kind they are." The key is to endure the pain and learn the lessons of self-discipline without losing the identity that is the spark of the girl or the original nation. Those who learn from pain will be rewarded with authority—"Katy, sitting upstairs in her big chair, held the threads of the house firmly in her hands" (chapter 11).

What Katy Did reminds us that one purpose of the Backfisch narrative is to heal the protagonist. In this example, the protagonist is not just physically awkward; she literally loses control of her body. Katy has to be injured physically to be healed emotionally and spiritually. Only then can she return to physical health. Katy becomes "the heart of the family" because of her literal need to retreat to an inner room of her home. In that interior space, she heals her own heedlessness and her family's wound from the loss of their mother. Her story models a process of healing and provides a narrative that defines pain as productive, an escapist fantasy that might well be attractive to post–Civil War readers.

Lenore must also take responsibility for her own education in a process of self-forming that is both painful and beneficial. In search of a "new life," she asks Herr Helldorf to be her tutor and commits herself to her own transformation. She writes:

> From this time I studied unweariedly. At first, indeed, the pen was often tossed under the table, and I ran off into the forest with a throbbing head and eyes filled with tears; but I always returned with a sigh, and slowly picked up the small steel tyrant from the floor, and worked away until at last my hard labour brought forth results. (293)

One result is the narrative we are reading; without conquering her dislike of writing, Lenore would not have been able to tell her story. And writing, it turns out, is also a metaphor for a more significant education. Just as Katy's "long year of schooling had taught her self-control" (chapter 11), Lenore finds that although it has "gone hard" with her, she has "conquered [her]self" (301).

Lenore's future husband, Herr Claudius, also speaks of pain positively. After he is injured rescuing Lenore's father from a burning house, Lenore tells him, "I know you are in pain, you are hurt! Oh Herr Claudius, how you must repent taking my father and myself into your house." As "an almost sunny smile for one moment chased away the expression of suffering that contracted his brows," he replies, "I can hardly admit that, Lenore. I recognize the wisdom of the Providence that leads us through various stages of experience before we attain Paradise" (363). Herr Claudius's injury is caused by heroism rather than disobedience, but like Katy, he sees his pain as a source of later, greater good.

As adolescent heroines, Katy and Lenore provide an alternative to the model of the suffering child and paradigm of inevitable growth. Unlike the vulnerable child, the adolescent heroine has the potential to transform herself and others. She is not merely paying a penalty, like the suffering child; she is engaged in necessary and productive change. The hard work required of the adolescent protagonist demonstrates that virtue and maturity are not inevitable evolutionary processes, but accomplishments that must be imagined and earned—lessons crucial to nations as well as to adolescents.

Making Women, Making Nations

One morning after the fall that injures Katy's back and confines her to bed, she tells her father her legs "feel so queer . . . just like the Prince's legs which were turned to black marble in the Arabian Nights" (chapter 9). She asks whether he thinks they will "feel natural" again soon. Here Katy defines "natural" through an origin story of past experience. Her active, bruised legs are defined as "natural" because they were familiar; her current experience of legs that feel like "black marble" is foreign, despite their link to a literary image. This example points to one way the Backfisch novel highlights the tension between a familiar past and an (as yet) unnatural present.

The Little Moorland Princess suggests one response to this problem: that the adolescent girl can become civilized without losing the natural qualities that make her charming. She thus provides a model for the nation that must preserve its authentic, original identity as the machinery of statehood advances. When he proposes, Herr Claudius says to Lenore, "Keep those innocent, childlike eyes,—they are my pride, my life" (403). Lenore learns to distinguish between fiction and reality, she learns to care for others, she learns to write in a beautiful script, and she learns to make sense of her life by telling us her story in the form of this narrative. All of these are skills that make her ready to assume her role in the great social household. But what makes Lenore desirable is the childlike nature that was apparent in the first pages of the book, when she stood barefoot in a stream. Herr Claudius's love of Lenore rests in his first glimpse of her barefoot on the moor. He encourages Lenore's journey from awkward child to competent mother and author but not at the expense of her "individuality." He tells her, "I told you at the first that the wayward, antagonistic element in your nature would have to be subdued—it distorts a truly feminine character, admired though it be by many as lawless grace,—but not an iota of your individuality must be disturbed" (303).

And yet, just as Katy is literally injured in the process of learning to be "The Heart of the House," Lenore must reshape herself to prepare herself for her roles as wife and mother. This shaping is most apparent in two scenes—first, when Lenore first sees the girls who work for Herr Claudius labeling seed packets: "How I pitied the poor young things in that back room! How cruelly their wings had been clipped! Oh, yes, their 'untutored instincts' had been 'trained'" (201)—and again, when Lenore first sees Herr Claudius's conservatory and imagines it a fairy-tale palace: "I did not know that here was a piece of the tropics imprisoned in the midst of German vegetation; for me there then existed but two climes,—miracle and reality" (219). In time, Lenore herself writes labels for seed packets to earn money to support her aunt; she too, despite Herr Claudius's insistence that her individuality be preserved, becomes "imprisoned" by what Herr Claudius calls "mental self-conquest" (304). Ultimately, both Katy and Lenore give up the delightful innocence of childhood in the interest of forming healthy communities, in which the woman's self-control rather than the child's exuberance must dominate.

Fairy Tales of Growth?

The Little Moorland Princess is both gothic mystery and realist Backfisch novel: it is in this intersection that many of the tensions of

Lenore's move toward adult identity are resolved. The novel begins with a kind of panorama of Lenore's past, present, and future. We are given three images: "two small brown feet" (4–5), a pair of "stout and durable" shoes adorned with "brass-headed nails" (25–26), and "pearl-embroidered slippers" (25). The bare feet that wade in the stream point to Lenore's link to nature and childhood—a childhood that is interrupted by the appearance of strangers on the moor. The shoes that were her birthday present lie discarded next to the stream where she wades—these "stout and durable" shoes are meant to usher her into a practical womanhood for which she is not yet ready, and she will ultimately discard them in favor of the light slippers that allow her to engage in a fairy-tale romance. While Lenore's reading has given her one sort of education, it is in the move to the city and interaction with a wider circle of acquaintances that Lenore will learn to distinguish between the romance of fairy tales and the reality of adult life. She will wear light slippers, but as a member of the bourgeoisie rather than as a princess.

This narrative provides us with two ways of living in the world that mirror Bismarck's distinction between liberal thought and practical action. On the one side are characters who believe their own fantasies—especially Charlotte and Dagobert, the two wards of Herr Claudius, who craft an elaborate story about their heritage and decide they are related to royalty; Herr Eckhof, the bookkeeper, who uses his devout Christianity to justify oppression; and Herr von Sassen, Lenore's father, whose obsession with archeology prevents him from caring for his daughter. On the other side is Herr Claudius, whose kindness supports all of these other characters in spite of their obliviousness to his work. While despising his practical application, they are very willing to benefit from the financial resources he provides.

While Charlotte wants to believe she is a character in a gothic romance, the novel tells a different story. Charlotte tells Lenore that "This idea of an innate aristocracy can be no chimeara" (231). Charlotte is deceiving herself, and perhaps the reader, into thinking this is a sensation novel. In fact it is something much more prosaic—a Backfisch story.

Lenore's early reliance on fairy tale reading makes her susceptible to Charlotte and Dagobert's claims that they are related to royalty. They persuade Lenore to use her access to a secret set of rooms where they believe they will find documents that support their claim. They believe "the solution to the mystery was as clear as daylight" (279), but in a scene reminiscent of *Northanger Abbey*, the solution turns out not to be as clear as day, and in fact, the brother and sister have drawn entirely false conclusions. Their "solution to the mystery" is simply another delusion of grandeur. In fact, the mystery is not at all romantic, but simply a sordid story of parental abandonment.

The young people's exploration of the attic rooms exposes another illusion—that of the bookkeeper, whose usurious form of Christianity oppresses the other household servants. He decides the secret rooms in the Carolinenlust are haunted, having heard footsteps and a shriek. The reader knows what he heard was Lenore exploring the secret passage and discovering these rooms; his susceptibility to a supernatural explanation further undermines his status as a religious authority.

The illusion of romance further gives way to realism when Lenore hears the story of Herr Claudius's first lover. She tells us her "darling fairy-tales paled and lost their charm beside this true story" (287). Ten years after Bismarck's "Blood and Iron" speech and its call to practical preparedness over liberal rhetoric, Lenore reinforces this lesson. While fairy tales of secret aristocratic connections and romantic first loves are enticing, they pale beside the practicality of a life well lived, the development of useful skills, and relationships with those with economic rather than social or intellectual power. This novel replaces the blood of the aristocracy with the blood of action (Herr Claudius is willing to sacrifice his life in the service of others). It relies on the iron of money well spent in the service of building an economic empire, rather than supporting the church or the unworthy. It calls for a life of practical work turned toward the goal of building community over the romance of liberalism.

(De)Constructing Borders

What Katy Did and *The Little Moorland Princess* helped "teach people how they are connected to their nations," as Lloyd Cramer says of the cultural practices behind nationalism (2)—a role more obviously played by political speeches such as the Gettysburg Address and "Blood and Iron." However, these novels simultaneously call our attention to the paradox of the nationalist project. Nationalist views of the self as distinct from others are, as Cramer points out, "always already entangled with the differences they theoretically oppose. The meaning of "German," for example, emerges through interactions with the "French"; and the oft-invoked racial category "white" derives meaning from its relations to "black" or "brown" (21). Caroline Levander helps us see that "the nation is imaginatively created and sustained through racial principles" (4), and the novel itself often relies on repressing the other to restore order.

Readers might see the girl protagonist as reinforcing borders as she is integrated into a community that tells her that her whiteness and privilege are necessary to membership in that community and as she learns lessons that allow her to reproduce her culture. Nira Yuval-Davis explains that "the mythic unity of national 'imagined communities' which divides the world between 'us' and 'them' is maintained and ideologically reproduced by a whole system of what Armstrong (1982) calls symbolic 'border guards.' These 'border guards' can identify people as members or non-members of a specific collectivity" (23). While girl protagonists might serve this role, the two heroines I discuss here demonstrate that girls in these novels also serve as border crossers. That they can be acknowledged as successful women despite these crossings indicates that the girls' novel questioned as well as reinforced fictions of nationalism.

Many scholars have discussed how *What Katy Did* moves Katy from a tomboy phase to a period of illness and physical inactivity to a new maternal role as "heart of the house." At its most explicit level, this is the story of a girl who learns to be a good woman. But Katy's fall and the emotional and spiritual crisis it provokes don't take place until we are more than halfway through the novel, and Katy's childhood experiences are particularly significant as a model of border crossing. Before the final act of carelessness and disobedience that leads to Katy's fall from a swing and long period as an invalid, the novel takes us through a series of episodes that characterize Katy and probably provide much of the novel's appeal for young readers. Katy is adventurous, creative, ambitious, and curious about the world. This curiosity comes forth most clearly in the chapter "Intimate Friends," which both points to Katy's immaturity and poor judgment when it comes to accepting others at face value and also suggests a model of community-building at odds with xenophobia and isolationism.

Katy's intelligent, compassionate interest in those her community defines as other—her "propensity to fall violently in love with new people"—was "always getting her into scrapes," as the narrator tells us in chapter 6. However, the trouble Katy causes her aunt by being careless with her clothing and body is very different from her intelligent, compassionate interest in those who her community defines as other. Katy befriends "a small Irish child," whom she plans to adopt, "a queer old black woman," "twin sisters, daughters of a German jeweler," "an ash-man and a steam-boat captain," "Mrs. Sawyer's cook," "a bonnet-maker," "a thief in the town-jail," the daughter of a fruit-merchant, and the invalid wife of a counterfeiter. "Ever since she began to walk and talk, 'Katy's intimate friends' had been one of the jokes of the household.'" Aunt Izzie is dismayed and "cried with mortification" when she learns Katy has been "visiting in a counterfeiter's family." Although Aunt Izzie believes Katy's father is "very particular about whom [she] make[s] friends with," in this instance, "Dr. Carr only laughed. He told Aunt Izzie that he didn't think that kind of crime was catching."

Aunt Izzie might critique Katy's willingness to cross the boundaries of class and race, and her father might laugh at it as charming, but her compassion shows the "before" picture of Katy as not altogether negative. She may be sloppy and disobedient and wild, but she is also loving. This points to a central tension the novel explores: How can the individual become civilized and take on adult roles in a wider community without losing the instinctual humanity of her childhood?

Through this border crossing, Katy learns to be "gentle and patient" long before the accident that forces immobility and sends her to "The School of Pain" (chapter 6). This novel proposes two models of emotional maturity—one comes through pain, the other through openness to difference, which is framed as a kind of mothering. While Aunt Izzie takes care of the children's physical needs—and later nurtures Katy in her illness—it is Cousin Helen who models the perfect loving mother, though she has no children of her own. When she first comes to visit, Cousin Helen "hugged them all round, not as if it was polite to like them because they were relations, but as if she had loved them and wanted them all her life" (chapter 7). Held in a warm embrace, the children feel significant and accepted.

Perhaps those on the outskirts of Katy's community feel similarly. Katy's genuine interest in everyone she meets makes her an idealized maternal figure before she is formally transformed by her loss of physical power. She may not yet know how to be gentle and considerate, but she is interested in everyone she meets and welcomes them into her encircling attention. But the last of these friends—Imogen Clark—is ultimately defined as unworthy of Katy's attention. Although Katy believes intuitively people are who they say they are, she must learn to temper this faith with good judgment and the realization that not everyone is to be trusted.

Similarly, the project of Lenore's adolescence is to learn to trust herself and to discern whether she can trust those around her. While *The Little Moorland Princess* is structured as a romance—Lenore ultimately falls in love with and marries a powerful merchant—it is also a narrative that explores the tensions implicit in German attempts at unification. To what extent is unification about excluding those who are different? What role does Christianity have in a new, united Germany? To what extent will the new empire be founded on the power of the aristocracy and intelligentsia, and to what extent will it be shaped by an educated merchant class?

The link between Lenore's ability to step into the role of daughter and her wider role as a member of the German community comes when she is taken to meet the princess at court. Princess Margarethe "is said to be especially kind of young, shy, and, forgive me for adding, rather silly girls, who are afraid upon the occasion of their first presentation at court" (142). While Lenore appears to have every advantage—as Charlotte puts it, she is fortunate in "an ancient name, a distinguished father, and a mother who was once in attendance at court!" (142)—this novel is not the story of Lenore's profit from any of these hereditary honors, but rather that of the story of the self-awareness that makes her ready to enter a productive life as a member of the bourgeoisie. Her power comes from a combination of her intrinsic good nature and what she learns to contribute.

In her first real conversation with her grandmother, who lies on her deathbed, Lenore feels the "mysterious tie of blood between grandmother and grandchild" (53) and is filled with a sense of "true affection for the whole world" (58). Lenore, who hardly knew her parents and has been raised by devoted servants, feels for the first time a sense of familial love. This grandmother, whose "oriental profile" (24) seemed so foreign, now appears as a link to a loving past. Lenore is handed "the last relic of the Jacobson splendor" (61)—a priceless pearl necklace—with the words "It belongs to your face, my child!" "The trinket has been a witness of much family affection and happy, peaceful times of comfort. It also fled from the stake and the persecution of Christian intolerance!" (61). As Lenore learns of her family's persecution, she is forced to question her own Christian experience. The world, it turns out, is far more complicated than Lenore's own experience or her beloved fairy tales suggest.

As the novel begins, Lenore is shown to be a natural child who notes without judgment her brown skin and learns to love her Jewish grandmother. Upon moving to the city for an education, however, Lenore is embarrassed by the contrast between her brownness and the white hands of her new companions, and she learns to hide her Jewish identity. Away from the natural moors, Lenore's fairy tales appear to come to life, and she assumes the "dazzling white forehead" (78) and "slender white fingers" (307) she sees are markers of romance and virtue.

Readers might expect Lenore's education will reinforce white supremacy—that the civilizing experience of town life will fade her skin while smoothing her rough manners.[1] As she says herself, "My nonsense-filled head, my brown hands that would not knit, and my unconquerable predilection for running barefooted, were the fearful features of the picture which two years of culture it was hoped would obliterate" (118). Instead, Lenore learns not that her hands are "brown and ugly," but that good character is not necessarily linked to whiteness (128). Lenore's fairy tale–fueled desire for whiteness is undermined by experience and careful mentorship.

Again and again, the novel links whiteness to deception. Lenore learns the "white hand" of the "gorgeous officer" (187) whose portrait she admires had "shattered the smooth brow by a single pressure upon the deadly trigger" (187). In the same way, the moral dissoluteness of those described as "white" shatters the fairy tale of white perfection. Lenore discovers that even her Aunt Christine, whom she has previously imagined as "a graceful maiden of one of my story-books, falling upon her knees, and extending her white arms in imploring entreaty" (67) is a sham; this discovery helps Lenore to value her own dark skin. She tells us: "My dark complexion, although fresh and clear, did not shine, in contrast with my aunt's smooth, white brow,—but to-day for the first time I saw the disgusting paint that was thick on some parts of her face" (382).

Those who grow pale in *The Little Moorland Princess* are responding to illness or shock, not to self-improvement, and as the narrative progresses, whiteness becomes linked to evil. The novel reveals Herr Eckhof, who initially appears to be the model of religious propriety, as a hypocrite: "An evil look was shot at the speaker from beneath those white eyebrows" (167). The young man whose white, smooth forehead Lenore idolizes turns out to be "false ... his chestnut curls wreathed above his brow like serpents" (263). Lenore fears her aunt will deceive Herr Claudius as she herself was deceived. She tells us, "I should not have allowed those white hands to touch him, and then the charm of the evil spell might have been broken" (398). As it turns out, Herr Claudius doesn't need her warning; he sees for himself that Christine is "hateful, painted sin" (402) in a scene that completes Lenore's education in the risks of fairy-tale fantasies. Whiteness lures her to see virtue where there is only selfishness and intolerance. Instead, Lenore must accept both her brown skin and her Jewish identity.

In *What Katy Did*, Katy appears to accept difference in others instinctively. Her task is to learn the self-control that will let her behave like a mother and thereby put her innate acceptance of others into practice. In *The Little Moorland Princess*, part of Lenore's own growth is in coming to accept her own differences—she is both Jew and Christian, aristocrat and commoner, natural and educated. She must publicly acknowledge her Jewish ancestry to move from the natural space of her childhood to the city and her role as the wife of a prominent merchant.

While Katy's original charm is linked to her lack of concern for social difference, she becomes focused on those most like her as she is isolated from the outside world and learns to fulfill her role as "heart of the home." Lenore, in contrast, moves from a private, isolated space in the country to a public role as a wife and author. She is able to do so, as the novel makes explicit, because she is willing to adopt the values of a new German middle class and embrace her complicated heritage. At one level, the apparent smoothness with which girls in these novels transform into women reinforces the notion that all members of the nation embrace a common goal. Even the least significant member of the nation—the girl—recognizes the need to move from nature to culture, to exercise self-control and to take her place in a national community. But the Backfisch story is not only about the miraculous and mysterious transformation of an unformed individual into a mature individual. It also reveals the messiness of the self that needs to be controlled and highlights the ways the girl's nature embraces (rather than excludes) the other. The Backfisch novel thus exposes both the illusion of national coherence and the ways self and other are entangled.

These stories of growing up are enmeshed in national fantasies of growing into mature power. They explore the interplay of love and pain and strategies for using pain as a force for maturation rather than bitterness, they acknowledge the significance of freedom and the need to regulate it, and they negotiate the issue of borders and the tension between inclusion and exclusion. Read side by side, *What Katy Did*, *The Little Moorland Princess*, the Gettysburg Address, and "Blut und Eisen" suggest the work of nation-building worked hand-in-hand with the work of educating adolescent girls. The girls' book helps girls accept the work of womanhood; nation-building inspires individuals to be willing to do the work of citizenship. Together, these texts tell the story of the work of coming of age in the 1860s and '70s and paint a picture of countries imagining a way out of the chaos of adolescence toward mature identities.

By depicting adolescent protagonists doing important physical and emotional work ("for want of a nail the kingdom was lost") and by showing pain and difference as providing opportunities, these novels give girls a way to see themselves as powerful actors. These novels construct female adolescence as a model that matters—certainly to girls and their families, but also potentially to wider communities that seek to form mature identities. In the next chapter, I look more closely at a specific experience of pain—homesickness—to understand how the Backfisch narrative is distinct from later girls' fiction. While the Backfisch narrative imagines a world in which adolescence is valuable and the work girls do matters both practically and metaphorically, the later girls' book moves toward more passive models of girlhood.

· CHAPTER FIVE ·
The Homesick Heroine

The girl heroine celebrated in Anglo-American girls' fiction is often characterized by her charming innocence and ability to change her community for the better. While this heroine may need to learn to curb her spirit and redefine her dreams as she takes on womanly roles, our love for her originates in the free spirit whose essential nature needs no refinement. The girl heroine in this model encourages adult readers to glorify childhood as a time of freedom and to celebrate girlhood as the pinnacle of female power while simultaneously teaching girl readers they must be feminine in order to be loved.[1] And yet, as Marah Gubar persuasively argues in *Artful Dodgers* about British Golden Age fiction, child protagonists are not necessarily passive recipients of adult desire and children's literature is not necessarily nostalgic. By identifying the Backfisch story as a distinct subgenre of girls' fiction, we can see that the path from the sentimental novel for women to the late nineteenth- and early twentieth-century orphan girl novel for girls (both of which rely on the rags-to-riches story of an orphan girl left to fend for herself in an initially hostile world) was interrupted by a group of novels that took messy adolescence rather than perfect girlhood as their topic. By so doing, they interrupt an assumption that the optimistic world of the girls' novel necessarily celebrates the past and privileges the child as object rather than subject.

Understanding the Backfisch book helps us make sense of the popular girls' books that followed. With this chapter, I investigate the trope of homesickness in the Backfisch book and then explore how the trope shifts with the Swiss novel *Heidis Lehr- und Wanderjahre* (*Heidi: Her Years of Wandering and Learning. A Story for Children and Those Who Love Children*).[2] I argue that as the girls' book moves away from focusing on an adolescent heroine, it shifts the responsibility for healthy communities from women to girls. When the idea of protected adolescent space no longer exists, the room to make mistakes also vanishes. The playful, experimental Backfisch period is replaced by an environment of neglect in which the girl must cultivate relationships in order to survive.

In her essay on *The Wide, Wide World*, Sara Quay talks about the importance of homesickness and nostalgia in mid-nineteenth-century America, where the idea of "home" was fraught because both citizens and immigrants were willing to leave their communities in search of opportunity. As a result, Quay argues, material objects took on a new significance as the carriers of emotion and as recompense for the loss that accompanies modern life. Quay suggests the book itself became a repository for emotions, including a longing for home. Novels like *The Wide, Wide World* "encouraged their readers to feel nostalgia . . . in order to overcome those same feelings" (54). One record of the link between the object and emotional attachment is expressed through the inscriptions that appear on the flyleaves of many of my copies of nineteenth-century girls' books. Take, for example, the copy of *Heidi* on my bookshelf. The book, a hardcover, peach-colored text with an idyllic image of a young girl on a mountain surrounded by cheerful goats, is triply inscribed. In 1910, Esther Bacher writes, "Best wishes for a happy birthday to Katherine"; in 1955 Katherine Philips gives this book to her granddaughters Marcia and Sandra; and in 1970 Carol Philips's name appears with the date. There is the fragment of a story here, of women who believe a book is an attractive gift, who draw attention to previous and future readers of the book through inscriptions, and who may see the book as a tool of emotional connection through an idealized past. The girls' books I discuss here were tremendously popular, perhaps because they served as a point of connection by reminding the adult of her own childhood (reading) and suggest the possibility of connection to a new generation.

While Quay sees the goal of the sentimental novel as to help adult readers to move past nostalgia through emotional catharsis, the girls' book has typically been seen as idealizing girlhood. As Anne Scott MacLeod provocatively argues, nineteenth-century girls' books foster longing for the freedom and potential of childhood that adolescence painfully erases, even while their characters pretend the transition to adult responsibilities is smooth. MacLeod uses texts from *Caddie Woodlawn* to *Rebecca of Sunnybrook Farm* to conclude that "women's sense of loss fed the nostalgia for childhood that children's books often expressed" (28). From this perspective, the girls' book both exposes and compensates for the pain of growing up; it fosters nostalgia by emphasizing the joys of childhood and the restriction of maturity.

Thus the girls' book can be read as about meeting adult needs and reinforcing social norms, both in the gendered ideologies it lays out and in its imagined ideal child. It is complicit in definitions of the child as innocent and passive; it serves the desires of adults to romanticize the past as a way of avoiding the discomforts of the present. The question seems to me to be one of pleasure and the source of satisfaction readers feel. Is the desire to read and reread girls' books and pass them along about idealizing stagnant girlhood and reinforcing restrictive gender structures, or is it about participating in narratives of change and growth? Probably both impulses are at play. What I will suggest here is that one way to make sense of the pleasure of the early girls' book is to look at discomfort—in particular, the experience of homesickness.

Backfisch novels take the heroine's departure from home as their starting place, suggesting the loss of home is key to the heroine's development. Although the Backfisch book would appear to be a prime candidate for the kind of nostalgic response critics suggest is so damaging to the actual child reader (and perhaps the adult reader as well), in fact it rejects nostalgia by explicitly examining homesickness and defining it as an appropriate but immature response. The child protagonist's education—and her resulting awareness that her homesickness stemmed from an incomplete understanding of her true needs—models a mature perspective for the adult who might be tempted to read these texts nostalgically.

In the Backfisch book, a loving community mentors the girl protagonist through adolescence. She does not have to earn the love of the adults around her; they see her innate value and teach her to work as a way of supporting her own growth. Despite its conservative, patriarchal framework, the Backfisch book honors both the free space of adolescence and the value of the adolescent girl. It suggests there is a period in life to make mistakes and still be loved, still be essentially virtuous. The messy, embodied girl learns to control her mind and body; womanhood becomes aligned with agency. Later novels—starting with *Heidi*, extending to the classic girls' books of the early twentieth century, and continuing to mid-twentieth-century adolescent fiction—return to a sentimental model in which the protagonist clashes with the adults in her life. Her relationship with them highlights a society at odds with itself. Instead of celebrating the girl protagonists' growing self-control and maturity, later novels romanticize the girl who remains cheerful and innocent despite the neglect or abuse of adults around her, suggesting female power lies in a lack of self-consciousness.

One way Backfisch books resist the adult reader's nostalgic impulse and the girl reader's passivity is by developing the theme of homesickness. Although the *Oxford English Dictionary* lists homesickness as a synonym for nostalgia, these books' depiction of homesickness can serve as an antidote to nostalgia for an unselfconscious girlhood. The term *homesickness* (or *heimweh*) was first known to be used by the Swiss Johann Keyssler in his 1758 *Travels through Germany* and is defined by the OED as "a depressed state of mind and body caused by a longing for home during absence from it; nostalgia." Homesickness or nostalgia is a disease of the mind and the body; it occurs during physical separation from a place that can be returned to, and was especially, in the earliest uses, a disease of Swiss mountaineers who longed to return to their mountains. This use of the term extended to soldiers in the US Civil War; as Susan

Matt writes, "Between 1861 and 1866, 5,213 white Union soldiers and 324 black soldiers suffered homesickness acutely enough to come to a doctor's attention; fifty-eight white and sixteen black soldiers died of the disease" (76–77).

The term *nostalgia* was defined initially as a synonym for homesickness. In the course of the nineteenth century, its definition shifted to include "sentimental longing *for* or regretful memory of a period of the past, esp. one in an individual's own lifetime; (also) sentimental imagining or evocation of a period of the past" (*OED*, italics in orig.). As Linda Hutcheon explains in her essay "Irony, Nostalgia, and the Postmodern," "by the nineteenth century, a considerable semantic slippage had occurred, and the word began to lose its purely medical meaning.... nostalgia became less a *physical* than a *psychological* condition; in other words, it became psychically internalized" (194, italics in orig.). Nostalgia thus moved its focus from the body to the mind, from actual experience and places to imagined worlds.

Hutcheon further argues that nostalgia, like irony, "is not something you 'perceive' *in* an object; it is what you 'feel' when two different temporal moments, past and present, come together for you and, often, carry considerable emotional weight" (199). Hutcheon's distinction between perception and feeling seems key to me; nostalgia, like homesickness, is controlled by the emotions rather than by reason. But while nostalgia implies a looking back from a distance and a sentimental response, homesickness is a response to two closely related temporal moments—"yesterday I was at home, today I am away"— and is enacted in physical illness. I'll go a step further and suggest nostalgia is an adult response, homesickness a child's response.

Homesickness in the Backfisch Novel

Clementine Helm's 1863 *Gretchen's Joys and Sorrows* sets up a pattern that appears again and again in the Backfisch novel. The girl protagonist leaves home and is overwhelmed by loss. She responds by exposing herself physically and emotionally through tears. However, her loss is more imagined than real; she still has a home and loving family and is welcomed by other loving adults. Thus her mentors encourage her to control her emotions and focus on her education. The Backfisch learns self-control and the proper use of a handkerchief; her appearance and intellectual capacity improve; and she finds she can create community for herself, even away from the physical space of her family of origin. Thus, in the Backfisch novel, self-control is not about repressing painful feelings (as it is for heroines from Ellen Montgomery to Pollyanna), but about the ability to create what Milton's Adam calls in Book XII of *Paradise Lost* "a paradise within." By reshaping her ideas about leaving home, the girl heroine reshapes her emotional experience.

We meet Gretchen at her teary departure from her childhood home: "Weeping, I once more embraced my father and mother, kissed again all my dear brothers and sisters, and shook hands with the assembled servants; then, sobbing, I drew myself back into the corner of the carriage, but immediately after leaned forward to wave my handkerchief, wet with tears, from the window" (1). That night, in a strange bed for the first time, Gretchen tells us: "Tear after tear rolled down upon the white pillow, and a feeling of homesickness oppressed my heart" (5). Rather than sentimentally recalling her childhood, Gretchen physically manifests the loss of home. Her homesickness is offset by her relationship with her aunt, whose affection makes her feel less distant from her family. Her aunt also models perfect womanhood, reminding Gretchen and the reader of the need for and purpose of this separation from her family and home. Gretchen is hardly an idealized child—her tears are messy rather than sentimental, her lack of manners awkward rather than charming. Gretchen spends much of the first part of the novel blushing in embarrassment as she learns she must not immerse her bread in her cup of coffee, embrace her friend on the street, or too actively befriend a young man. Restraint and forethought are to be her watchwords—a proper young woman is self-controlled, graceful, and above all, extremely clean.

Thus the reader is hardly surprised when Gretchen realizes separation from home is a blessing, not a trial. She says, "the separation had not made me sick, and I had not pined away as I thought.

No; on the contrary, I bloomed in all the freshness and vigor of youth—had become stronger, and if my mirror told me the truth, much improved in appearance" (102). Gretchen comes to celebrate her maturity. As narrator, she redefines the freedom of childhood as social awkwardness, inferior to the life of a civilized young lady. While Gretchen enjoyed her unfettered childhood, when she was "permitted to do as [she] pleased," she now realizes maturity is far more satisfying (9). The Backfisch novel both recognizes homesickness as intensely painful and depicts it as subject to reason. Gretchen tells us: "For a long time I had not felt that longing which had at first so unspeakably tormented me, for my dear father's house. I understood better and better how well for my intellectual development it was for me to spend a part of my youth with Aunt Ulrike" (39). Gretchen's mature understanding transforms her emotional response to being in Berlin. It is not that she continues to feel pain, but is willing to suffer for the sake of an education; it is that understanding itself transforms her embodied response to being in Berlin.

Other Backfisch novels also use tears to mark the heroine's starting point of emotional excess and immaturity. When Lucy in *The Flower of the Family* leaves home, not only does she cry, but her whole family is "in tears, for this was the first parting they had ever known" (100). As Lenore describes her parting from "the paradise of [her] childhood" in *The Little Moorland Princess*, she tells us that "the floodgates of my tears . . . broke forth with unrestrained passion" (60). In *What Katy Did at School*, the sequel to *What Katy Did*, when Katy's younger sister Elise goes to stay overnight with family friends in chapter 1, she finds "as often as the thought of home and Katy and papa came, a wild longing to get back to them would rush over her, and her eyes would fill again with sudden tears." Her father has the good sense to anticipate her homesickness and comes to take her home after just a few days—Elise, it is clear, is not yet old enough to benefit from an extended journey from home.

Elise's authentic response is set in contrast to a theatrical demonstration by the character Lilly in chapter 3. Lilly sobs hysterically: "I shall be so homesick! It will kill me; I know it will. Please let me stay." The scene makes it clear Lilly is merely performing grief; her tears embarrass Katy, who had "been used to considering tears as things to be rather ashamed of," to hold back or hide. Katy's maturity comes not from being away from home, but from the "long year" as an invalid that "taught her self-control" in *What Katy Did* (chapter 11). While Katy initially resists her change in situation, she learns not to wallow in images of her adventurous past, but to be content with her current reality. Significantly, Katy's emotional healing takes place before her physical healing. Her self-control helps her be happy and a blessing to others, regardless of how much pain she experiences. Like the other Backfisch heroines I discuss here, Katy is able to benefit from losing her childhood freedom because of the community of loving adults who continue to care for her.

Lenore learns the same lesson as we watch her shift from violent emotion to self-control. She tells Herr Claudius: "I long so for the Dierkop! Sometimes I suffer so with longing that I could dash my head against all these trees!" (171). She learns she must be educated and that she had been "so terribly ignorant on the moor" (173). Similarly, Ilse in Emmy von Rhoden's *An Obstinate Maid* mourns the loss of an unfettered childhood; she experiences violent grief in her first weeks at boarding school. As Ilse learns to govern her temper, she rejoices in a new feeling of freedom in having "won a victory over her stubborn spirit" (111). Ilse quickly learns that mastery of her temper is the key to true happiness. While she longs to return to the place of her birth, she no longer wishes to be an uncivilized child.

An Obstinate Maid further undermines nostalgia through Fräulein Gussow's story. As a young woman, Fräulein Gussow rejected her lover out of a stubborn sense of pride, a decision that cost her both happiness and physical comfort. She looks back at the past with regret and even nostalgia: "Her childhood, her young adulthood, stood clearly before her. What had happened to her hopes, her dreams? All was destroyed—and it was her own fault!" (140). Fräulein Gussow's regret—her longing for a past before she made her big mistake—defines nostalgia as a response to error. She grieves as a result of looking back and knowing she could have made a better choice; if she had made the right choices, there would be no need for nostalgia. According to this novel, proper education may

She threw herself upon a chair by the window, and wept aloud—Page 91

"She threw herself upon a chair by the window, and wept aloud." *An Obstinate Maid* (Philadelphia: George W. Jacobs, 1898), 91.

require a period of homesickness but will result in a life free from the insidious pull of nostalgia.

The Flower of the Family echoes this theme, framing Lucy's time in the city as a "necessary season of refreshment and repose" (167). Lucy longs to be with her family and worries she is neglecting her duty by leaving her mother "just when [she is] becoming useful" (207). Lucy sees her worth to her family in terms of the labor she can provide; she imagines she is valuable because she is "useful." Her parents see the situation differently; they are willing to give up her much-needed service at home to provide a sort of retreat space where her own development is primary, a free space of exploration and self-development from which to take on her role as wife and mother. Although *The Flower of the Family* suggests service is the primary goal of a woman's life, it acknowledges this service is ideally the work of women rather than girls. Lucy's father insists she take this time in the city "to grow young again" (113). *The Flower of the Family* defines home not as a magical space of innocence and pleasure, but as one of domestic drudgery, from which Lucy (the Backfisch) is relieved in order to grow toward a more complex identity.

Together, these books suggest allowing ourselves to feel homesick means allowing physical and emotional symptoms to dominate over our reason; these heroines learn not to make that mistake. Gretchen may regret the loss of childhood ignorance, but she learns girlish sloppiness is more embarrassing than pleasant. Katy may mourn the loss of physical freedom, but she delights still more in her role as "The Heart of the House." Ilse may feel confined by the rules of boarding school life and the restrictions of feminine clothing, but she understands these restrictions—and the need to control her temper they represent—will ultimately lead to happiness. These stories push us to see homesickness as a childish emotion to be overcome, not as a dangerous symptom of the adult nostalgia for childhood.

Homesickness in Other Girls' Novels

Although homesickness is a theme throughout the different iterations of the girls' book (as well as the sentimental novel), various types of girls' books handle it differently. In the family story, homesickness marks femininity rather than immaturity. Since the family is at the heart of these novels, it makes sense that a longing for home would actually be a positive quality. In *Little Women*, for example, Amy goes on what could loosely be termed a Backfisch journey when she travels to Europe with Aunt March. The homesickness she feels when away is not a sign of immaturity; instead it makes her more desirable and more womanly.

> She was sitting here that day, leaning her head on her hand, with a homesick heart and heavy eyes, thinking of Beth, and wondering why Laurie did not come. She did not hear him cross the court-yard beyond, nor see him pause in the arch-way that led from the subterranean path into the garden. He stood a minute, looking at her with new eyes, seeing what no one had ever seen before—the tender side of Amy's character. (270)

Similarly, when Beth imagines her own death, she tells Jo, "I'm not afraid, but it seems as if I should be homesick for you even in heaven" (197). The novel does not criticize Beth for her perspective or suggest her lack of trust in the afterlife is a sign of immaturity. The family story elevates the cohesive family above other desires or goals; Amy's and Beth's longing for home is a marker of Marmee's success.

Professor Bhaer takes the role of homesickness a step further. His growing attachment to Jo is framed by "heimweh":

> But after the boys were abed, he sat long before his fire, with the tired look on his face, and the "heimweh" or homesickness lying heavy at his heart. Once when he remembered Jo, as she sat with the little child in her lap, and that new softness in her face, he leaned his head on his hands a minute, and then roamed about the room, as if in search of something that he could not find. (176)

Professor Bhaer's longing may be related to his loss of his homeland, but this passage explicitly links it to an imagined future, not to the past. The passage also links his longing for home to "that new softness" in Jo's face, a softness that makes her desirable and that allows him to imagine her as a wife and mother rather than as a girl.

The orphan girl novel links homesickness with despair because the home that is longed for is forever gone. The project of these novels is to create a new family home, a space from which the girl can journey and return. When, early in *Anne of Green Gables*, Anne learns Matthew and Marilla had planned to adopt a boy, not a red-headed girl, she sobs:

> "You don't want me!" she cried. "You don't want me because I'm not a boy! I might have expected it. Nobody ever did want me. I might have known it was all too beautiful to last. I might have known nobody really did want me. Oh, what shall I do? I'm going to burst into tears!" (chapter 3)

Although Anne's tears are familiar to readers of Backfisch books, their cause is new. Like the Backfisch, the orphan girl goes on a journey, but unlike the Backfisch, she doubts her welcome when she arrives—and so do we. She is given a place to live out of a sense of duty (Rebecca, Pollyanna) or so she can contribute to the household (Anne). She has no loving family behind her and arrives where she is unknown and also unloved. She has reason to cry; as Anne says, "YOU would cry, too, if you were an orphan and had come to a place you thought was going to be home and found that they didn't want you because you weren't a boy" (chapter 3). The Backfisch, in contrast, is older and ready to travel. She cries because she wants the security of being loved as a child and resists the need to be educated. Her longing for home is childish—and she is no longer a child.

By the time Anne leaves her home in Green Gables for school, her story begins to look like a Backfisch novel: she does at that point have a loving home, and she leaves, like the Backfisch, to receive an education she can't get at home. Her tears also replicate those of the homesick Backfisch. Installed in her boardinghouse room, Anne is overwhelmed by "the first agony of homesickness that seized upon her," attempts to control her tears, and then succumbs to them, saying, "I can't cheer up—I don't WANT to cheer up. It's nicer to be miserable!" (chapter 34). The narrator here has more sympathy for Anne's homesickness than do earlier narrators, and makes this point by putting a critique of Anne's homesickness in the mouth of an unlikeable character. "'You've been crying,' remarked Josie, with aggravating pity. 'I suppose you're homesick—some people have so little self-control in that respect'" (chapter 34). Here Josie sounds like Katy as she calls up the language of self-control. Unlike the Backfisch, whose secure identity within a family makes her homesickness a sign of immaturity, Anne's homesickness reinforces the triumph that she now has a home for which to be homesick. Like a good Backfisch, Anne does not allow her longing for a real home to overset her educational goals; she quickly finds herself happy and busy at Queen's Academy.

Anne of Green Gables redefines tears as markers of emotional connection, linking it to the family story. Anne is not the only one who cries when she leaves home; the first night after Anne leaves, Marilla "buried her face in her pillow, and wept for her girl in a passion of sobs that appalled her when she grew calm enough to reflect how very wicked it must be to take on so about a sinful fellow creature" (chapter 34). An evangelical novel might have supported Marilla's critique of her own tears, but *Anne of Green Gables* suggests that tears related to love are a sign of connection rather than immaturity. In a parallel scene, as Anne weeps for Matthew, Marilla tells her: "There—there—don't cry so, dearie. It can't bring him back. It—it—isn't right to cry so." Anne's response is the one endorsed by the novel: "Oh, just let me cry, Marilla," sobbed Anne. "The tears don't hurt me like that ache did" (chapter 37). In this novel, tears become not a mark of childishness or resistance to God's will, but a sign of womanly connection.

Anne's willingness to assert her own authority in the scene with Marilla points to a sense of self-possession based on her rich interiority. In an earlier scene, Marilla asks Anne:

"You don't chatter half as much as you used to, Anne, nor use half as many big words. What has come over you?"

> Anne colored and laughed a little, as she dropped her book and looked dreamily out of the window, where big fat red buds were bursting out on the creeper in response to the lure of the spring sunshine.
> "I don't know—I don't want to talk as much," she said, denting her chin thoughtfully with her forefinger. "It's nicer to think dear, pretty thoughts and keep them in one's heart, like treasures. I don't like to have them laughed at or wondered over." (chapter 31)

Anne has learned self-control and through that self-control constructed an interior space in which she can judge for herself. Anne's maturity is clearly a source of happiness rather than loss for her, linking her closely to the Backfisch. But while the Backfisch heroine has parents to construct a protected adolescent space for her, Anne must do this work for herself. Anne does acquire mentors, and shapes a community that can allow her a *Backfischzeit*, but her novel is unlike the traditional Backfisch novel in that it begins with Anne as a child rather than as an adolescent and shifts the responsibility for being loved onto Anne herself.

In recollecting and rereading Backfisch books, some adult readers might ignore the push for growth and focus on the longing for home. But these texts explicitly reject nostalgic reading even as they describe an idyllic past. Ironically, these novels pay homage to homesickness—and by implication, nostalgia—only to reject them as childish. Unlike the family story or orphan girl novel, Backfisch stories redefine the child's longing for home and the adult's longing for the past as partial vision. Once educated, the heroine may still love her home, but she will love the growth that separation from home allowed even better.

Heidi as a Moment of Transition

How do we get from the Backfisch book, with its secure adolescent heroine who is allowed a protected space in which to make mistakes, to early twentieth-century novels like *Anne of Green Gables*, in which the heroine must forge her own interior space in order to avoid critique? I propose Johanna Spyri's tremendously popular *Heidi* provides us with insight into that transition. *Heidi* is the best known in English of the German-language texts I discuss and one of the most popular children's books written in any language. Spyri began *Heidi* in the 1870s, as part of a project to help refugees who came to Switzerland as a result of the Franco-Prussian war.[3] Published as two volumes in Germany in 1880 and 1881, *Heidi* was an immediate best seller, was translated into English at least thirteen times between 1882 and 1959, and remains in print in multiple editions today.[4] While many Backfisch books were best sellers in their own countries, *Heidi* was the first novel for girls to be a best seller in both English and German and to remain in print in both languages. Published twenty years before the boom of the American orphan girl novel in the early twentieth century, *Heidi*—as a novel that looks both backward and forward—helps us see how the wider genre of the girls' book shifts from focusing on the girl's own education to her community's transformation. *Heidi* combines the structure of the Backfisch novel with an orphaned heroine and glorifies the natural world over city life.

Heidi demonstrates the transnational literary context of the nineteenth century. For a variety of reasons, including lax or nonexistent copyright laws, the translation and republication of books led to significant exchange as the genre of the girls' book was establishing itself. *Heidi* itself is a Swiss text that was influenced by earlier German girls' books. The German girls' book tradition was also influenced by American sentimental novels (including *The Wide, Wide World*, translated into German at least three times in the nineteenth century), and the girls' book is shaped in both countries by British novels for girls and women. *Heidi* was written at a time when the strong language boundaries in Switzerland meant that each region of the country was linked across borders by language. As a German-speaking Swiss, Spyri aligned herself from a literary perspective with the land we now call Germany; *Heidi* was published by a German publisher (F. A. Perthes in Gotha). In *Telling Tales: The Impact of Germany on English Children's Books: 1780–1918*, David Blamires identifies *Heidi* as an important influence on English-language girls' books. Recognizing this international literary exchange allows us a more nuanced vision of the history of the girls' book and complicates an assumption that the Anglo-American girls' book developed in an English-language vacuum.

While *Heidi*'s similarity to later girls' books has been discussed by critics from Perry Nodelman to Jerry Griswold to Monica Elbert, the novel's debt to the already existing genre of girls' fiction has not been described. Peter Skrine claims *Heidi* "had no direct or obvious model" (147); Joe Sutliff Sanders writes in his study of the classic orphan girl novel that "*Heidi* is so far removed from the Anglophone tradition of sentimentalism that I am hesitant to include it in this history" (7). Yet *Heidi* does in fact have much in common with one strand of the early girls' book—the Backfisch book—and uses its structure as a jumping-off point for a new kind of girls' book.

In his 1947 study of best sellers, Frank Mott acknowledges two "great outpourings" of novels that focus on the experiences of girls— the first in the mid-nineteenth century, the second in the early twentieth century (215–16). The girls' books Mott describes as belonging to the first outpouring fall into two categories—they are either family stories that show the development of individuals within the confines of a family circle (*Little Women, The Daisy Chain*), or Backfisch books that describe the development of an adolescent girl away from home (*The Flower of the Family, Faith Gartney's Girlhood, An Old-Fashioned Girl*). Whether a family story or a Backfisch book, the girls' book of the first period assumes a protected world that wants the girl to grow up successfully. At this point in literary history, the girls' book was separated from the novel for adults by the secure nature of the protagonist's world. In contrast, in books aimed at a juvenile audience in the second "outpouring," girl protagonists are sent into unsupportive environments where their childhood is idealized and they learn by suffering rather than through support (*The Little Princess, Anne of Green Gables, Pollyanna*). *Heidi* stands at a pivot point—before *Heidi*, best-selling novels for girls assume the protagonist can focus simply on her own growth; after *Heidi*, the children's book takes on the sentimental model of the girl child in danger and makes it her work to fix her world.

Heidi influences the later girls' book in at least two related ways—in the structure of the narrative and in its celebration of the natural world. *Heidi* shows us how we get from early girls' books (such as the Backfisch novel or family story) in which girls are safe to girls' books in which girls are vulnerable (the orphan girl novel). In the former, girls need only worry about their own education and marriage, and the natural world is a source of pleasure; in the latter, girls must change others, and the natural world becomes a vital space for healing. In the Backfisch book, mentors teach the adolescent girl domesticity and social skills so she can civilize the natural self. In contrast, the orphan girl novel imagines its young protagonist and her close link with nature as a vehicle for transforming her community. Like earlier heroines, Heidi is in need of a practical education and the guidance of a loving female mentor. Like later heroines, she is a vulnerable orphan and her natural innocence is seen as the antidote to a diseased world. Because of its tremendous popularity, *Heidi* created a new model that was repeatedly replicated in the early twentieth century—one that pulled together the sentimental novel for women and the Backfisch novel to create a new kind of girls' book—the orphan girl novel.

Heidi begins with the orphaned five-year-old Heidi being led up into the Swiss Alps to the Alm-Uncle's hut by her aunt. Aunt Dete has been offered a position in the city and needs to be relieved of the care of the young child—so she takes Heidi to her grandfather and informs them both that she is done being responsible. Despite this inauspicious beginning, Heidi loves the hut, the goats, and the mountains and quickly blossoms in this natural space. She accompanies Peter the goatherd into the mountains, learns to help her grandfather keep house, and befriends Peter's blind grandmother. Heidi, it would seem, has landed safely in the world. Though she is younger than typical girls' book protagonists at this point, she shares their confidence that adults will care for her. If we read *Heidi* as a Backfisch novel, the plot begins with Heidi's secure and loving home in the Swiss Alps, continues with her journey to the city for her own advancement, considers homesickness as a sign of immaturity, and emphasizes her growth as a literate Christian who returns home better able to serve her community.

Heidi immediately establishes a rapport with her misanthropic grandfather through her own unselfconsciousness; this is in fact one way Heidi distinguishes herself from Backfisch heroines. She is never embarrassed, doesn't even notice she may not be wanted, and has the assurance of a goat in a field of clover. Her close alignment with nature allows Heidi to disarm the suspicions of adults and win her grandfather's love and trust. But Aunt Dete returns, this time to take Heidi to Frankfurt, where she has secured a position for her as a companion to Klara, a wealthy girl who is an invalid.

When Heidi leaves her grandfather and her new home in the Alps, she appears to be following a typical Backfisch arc: she moves from the known and loved to an unfamiliar but necessary education. She experiences a loving mentor when Klara's grandmother comes to visit and teaches her to read, sew, and pray. Unlike Peter's grandmother in the Alps, who needs Heidi's care, Klara's grandmother keeps Heidi profitably employed and converses with her, allowing Heidi to feel understood and educated in the same space. But Klara's grandmother is only a visitor in the home. Lacking a constant female mentor, Heidi is not able to flourish emotionally or socially. Now Heidi looks more like the orphaned heroine of a sentimental novel—she is berated, isolated, and terribly homesick. On the verge of emotional and physical collapse, she is sent back to the Alps, where she regains her health, helps her grandfather return to a Christian community, teaches the goatherd to read, and cures her Frankfurt friend. Her education does not result in her own transformation; it leads her to transform those around her.

Heidi, it turns out, is no Backfisch. But her appropriation of the Backfisch storyline marks this novel as a pivotal transition point in the novel for girls. While she learns to pray, we get no sense of internal struggle or transformation in her. Like the stereotypically unquestioning child, she takes what she is told at face value, whether it is to her benefit or not. When Fräulein Rottmeier tells her she must not cry or tell anyone she is homesick, she obeys, and only reveals her distress through sleepwalking.

In many ways, homesickness drives the plot of this novel—a homesickness instigated by the beauty of the Swiss Alps and

A GRANDMAMMA. 147

still more about them. Heidi liked to look again and again at the green pasture and the shepherd in the midst of his flock, standing so contentedly, leaning on his long staff, for there he was still with his father's flock, following the merry lambs and goats, for this was his delight.

Then came the picture where he had run away from his father's house, and was in a strange land, obliged to tend the swine, and had grown very thin because he

had nothing but husks to eat. The sun no longer shone so golden in this picture, and the land looked gray and gloomy. But there was still another picture to the story, in which the old father, with outstretched arms, is coming out of the house and running to wel-

The young Heidi learning to read, *Heidi: A Little Swiss Girl's City and Mountain Life* (Boston: Ginn, 1899), 147.

augmented by Heidi's youth.[5] Taken from her mountain home to Frankfurt, she immediately feels closed in by the tall buildings of the city and wishes to return home to the open skies and mountains. Her longing for home ultimately manifests itself as physical illness and is correctly diagnosed by a kindly doctor: "She is suffering from homesickness so that she is reduced almost to a skeleton, and soon will be one, if this goes on" (319).

The many English translations of *Heidis Lehr- und Wanderjahr* all follow the German text in describing her homesickness with diagnostic precision and detail. Heidi becomes unable to eat; she dreams of her home; she feels a pressure like a great stone in her chest. Forbidden to cry, Heidi ultimately acts out her despair through sleepwalking. Once her employers recognize the extent of her suffering, they return her to the Alps and the "strengthening mountain air," which does indeed relieve her symptoms (320). It is easy to sympathize with Heidi's desire to return home, and to even fear blocking her return will result in her death. Heidi's illness is her only source of power once she is taken to Frankfurt. The text simultaneously appears to support Heidi's sentimental longing for her childhood freedom in the Alps and to affirm the power homesickness holds over both the heroine and the adults around her.

From this perspective, Heidi encourages a nostalgic response—the adult reader can empathize with Heidi's desire to return home and bask in a parallel desire to return to or idealize childhood. In fact, Heidi complicates a nostalgic reading, even if the text does not firmly reject one. For in Frankfurt, Heidi gains three things—the ability to read, a faith in God, and wealthy patrons—and the novel emphasizes that she would not have acquired these assets at home on the mountain. Living in the city does make Heidi sick, but the novel suggests her illness is justified by the education it allows her and the advantageous connections it provides. Heidi must suffer away from home so she can help those she loves—Peter's grandmother, for whom she can now buy soft bread; her grandfather, who returns to church and the community at her bidding; Klara, whose friendship with Heidi leads her out of her wheelchair and to a full recovery; and Peter, who learns to read with Heidi's tutoring.

Heidi pays a price for these gifts, but the novel insists—and Heidi agrees—her suffering is worthwhile. Heidi tells Klara: "Haven't you realized . . . what a good thing it is that the good God does not grant our prayers, no matter how earnestly we pray to him, if he has something better in store for us?" (210). So while her year in Frankfurt almost kills Heidi, the novel ultimately focuses on the "almost," and both Heidi and the narrator celebrate the good that comes out of her suffering. Heidi's "illness" disguises the good that will come from her lessons in the city and the patrons she gains. Spyri and her translators glorify the Swiss Alps and help us long for their beauty; they also work to convince us our own true home is heaven, and point us toward the future rather than the past.

Heidi is thus anti-nostalgic, but only because Heidi's physical illness is justified as a source of spiritual and community growth. Here Heidi is very different from Gretchen, Lucy, Lenore, or Ilse, whose stories focus on the girl's own development. She looks more like Katy, whose suffering and resulting education result in her being able to be "a mother to the little ones." But while Katy is twelve when the novel begins and sixteen when it ends, Heidi is seven when she is taken to Frankfurt. And while Katy is supported throughout her suffering by loving adults, the occasional appearance of Klara's kind grandmother serves mostly to underscore Heidi's vulnerability and lack of adult compassion.

Heidi stands at a point of divergence when the orphan girl heroine splits away from the adolescent heroine of earlier novels. As an orphan girl, she reimagines the heroine's relationship with nature and the constraints of culture. While earlier heroines must learn to clothe themselves in manners, Heidi literally tosses aside her clothes as she climbs the Alps. Perhaps this freedom comes because *Heidi* is decidedly not a romance. The early girls' novel relies on the frame of heterosexual romance to certify its heroine's successful maturation; *Heidi* demonstrates that the heroine of a girls' book can be maternal without growing up and can demonstrate success by transforming a community rather than by constructing a new family unit. Through all of this, *Heidi* established a formula so compelling that for many critics, this version of the girls' book would become a defining one.

Conclusion

In the Backfisch novel, the move to the city is an opportunity for education and maturation and leads to the girl's happiness and social success. But while Heidi is educated in her year in Frankfurt, she fades away physically rather than thriving. *Heidi* thus points toward an increasingly sharp divide between city and country, where the health-giving properties of the natural world must provide recompense for the corruption of city life. The term *nostalgia* was used not only to describe the homesickness of Swiss soldiers removed from the Alps but also later was used to describe the mental condition of girls sent to live in the city who became pyromaniacs and murderers as a way of returning home.[6] Like these debilitated soldiers and dangerous serving girls, Heidi's pain is manifest both inwardly and outwardly. Though her sleepwalking is less violent than wholesale murder, Heidi also disrupts her household. Her nightly wanderings lead the adults around her to believe a ghost or intruder is at work.

Heidi helps us think about what the orphan girl accomplishes for the girls' book that the protected adolescent does not. While the orphan girl had a clear role in earlier sentimental novels in creating intense emotional experience, the girls' book began as a genre that emphasized self-reliance and managing—not indulging—emotion. Heidi's vulnerability in the hostile environment of Frankfurt glorifies the natural world and suggests nature and lack of constraint are necessary to the girl's well-being and to her community's moral health. It also increases our awareness of the heroine's need to compensate for losing her mother by embracing the natural world. Earlier novels—both family stories and Backfisch books—describe girls who are well mothered and mentored; these girls don't need to replace the fantasy of the mother with the experience of nature. In these earlier novels, enjoying nature might be a marker of moral/spiritual development, but the goal is maturation and not reliance on the natural world. The city is usually framed as the ideal space for social growth.

This shift in the girls' book doesn't simply glorify nature; it also pushes readers toward sentimentality and passivity rather than self-reliance. The goal of reading becomes emotional indulgence rather than education and motivation. The girls' book regresses. It becomes the girl child's responsibility to heal her world and nature's responsibility to heal her. Adults are let off the hook here—rather than being responsible for helping the girl mature successfully, as they are in earlier girls' novels, they can sentimentalize the past and are not expected to fix their present. And perhaps this is the source of *Heidi*'s popularity. It allows adults to feel less responsible, less burdened by the work of educating children. That is the job of nature and of the child herself.

While earlier heroines of girls' books are closer to the agential children Marah Gubar describes in *Artful Dodgers* with a talent for pleasing themselves, Heidi seems determined simply to please others. And at this crossroads in the genre of the novel for girls, the Backfisch novel—with its adaptable adolescent heroine—is replaced by a child who seems oblivious to any desire but the simple "I want to go home." Orphaned before the novel begins, manipulated by the aunt who first raised her, Heidi is effortlessly cured by the mountain air. A child of nature, she directs the focus of the girls' novel away from self-development and toward community-building and the exaltation of nature. *Heidi*'s tremendous success spoke to something in adult desires to be saved by the natural child from the anxiety of adolescence, and her pattern became the central one in the classic girls' novel of the twentieth century.

· CONCLUSION ·
Loving Girls, Loving Growth

I began this project with the question of why I love girls' books, despite the restrictive images of femininity they portray. I've argued here that one reason these books speak powerfully to readers is because they depict girlhood as important and interesting. In particular, the subgenre of the Backfisch book draws our attention to the pleasure to be found in reading about girls who grow up in loving communities where the work of personal transformation is valued and supported and where the opportunities of a fluid identity are celebrated.

The Backfisch —the adolescent girl who paved the way for later literary heroines—opens a window into early structures for mentoring and protecting adolescent girls. Backfisch books, the earliest novels for girls to focus on female adolescence, challenge our cultural assumptions about progress, about adolescence, and about what it was like to be a girl in the nineteenth century. In particular, by imagining girls as powerful actors and adolescence as creative space, they complicate a belief that girls' books always evolve toward less sexist and restrictive images of girls.

The Backfisch helps us imagine female adolescence as a flexible space of growth, acknowledging adolescence differs from other stages of life and encouraging us to relax our notion of identity as constant. The Backfisch is both charming and awkward, selfish and empathetic. She makes mistakes—lots of them. The adults around her name this space of exploration—a *Backfischzeit*—and make it clear to her that she is loved regardless of her behavior, that she is safe physically even as her psychological landscape is in flux. In particular, she learns she is loved not just by her biological mother but also by other women and peers. The social dangers she faces are offset by connection with kind, powerful women who want to be part of her education and who recognize that the hard work of adolescence is not hers alone. Her mentors tell her that the choices she makes matter, that the mystery of transforming herself into a woman can be explained, learned, practiced. As she engages in the work of learning to perform femininity, she sees that her work makes an impact on her community. She uses her hands to create and clean; she uses language to describe her experience.

The Backfisch models flexible growth, an alternative to naïve childhood or stagnant adulthood. Her shifting identity resonates with stories of growth at the national level. Perhaps most significantly, as she learns new skills and strategies and begins successfully navigating an adult social network, mentors praise her growth rather than defining it as a loss. She is not stuck between her culture's desire for the girl child and her own embodied maturity; she can love her childhood experiences without longing to be a child.

Including the Backfisch novel in our history of girls' fiction not only changes the way we think about adolescence, it also leads to new interpretations of later girls' books. For example, the Backfisch narrative helps us see more clearly some of the conditions that lead to suffering and growth in contemporary novels such as *Sweet Whispers, Brother Rush* (1982), *Under the Mesquite* (2011), and *The Chaos* (2012).

Sweet, in Virginia Hamilton's *Sweet Whispers, Brother Rush*, is on the verge of adolescence; her life is changing. The boys on the street corner whistle at her, though they also acknowledge she isn't "ripe" yet. Through magical realism, Hamilton fleshes out Sweet's experience of coming to understand her past and accommodate her fears and hopes for the future. Like earlier Backfisch heroines, Sweet is proficient in the kitchen and easy to please; she nurtures her sibling.

But Sweet lacks consistent othermothers in addition to not having her own biological mother present. There is no one to direct Sweet's daily life, no one to assure her she is safe. In fact, Sweet's world is marked by risk, most clearly articulated when her brother dies because he doesn't receive appropriate medical attention. The novel's happy ending comes when Sweet's mother realizes Sweet needs to be nurtured and finds an adult woman to live with her.

Unlike the heroine of an orphan girl novel, Sweet has a mother; unlike the family story, in this narrative she is expected to run her own household. It is Sweet's inadequate environment—not raging adolescent hormones—that leads her to resent her mother, a resentment most clearly articulated through her plan to run away. A poor, inner-city Black girl, on the surface Sweet looks very different from the white middle- and upper-class girls of the nineteenth-century Backfisch novel. The novel shows she needs the same things: a protected space that allows for errors and the care and attention of adult women.

Guadalupe Garcia McCall's *Under the Mesquite* tells the story of Lupita, the oldest of six children, who experiences the death of her mother as she moves through adolescence. Lupita's story begins with her experience of racism in a Mexican-American community and ends when she leaves for college, with no thought of marriage in mind. As readers, we experience the psychological trauma of Lupita's loss of her mother far more intimately than we do the losses of the Backfisch protagonist. And yet Lupita's journey has much in common with those of earlier Backfisch protagonists: like them, she must learn to accommodate herself to a world she doesn't always understand. Lupita returns to her grandmother's home in Mexico to recover from the trauma of her mother's death. Like Lucy in *The Flower of the Family*, she is capable of managing the domestic work of the household like a mother, but her family recognizes she deserves a protected space to mourn and grow into adulthood.

On the surface, Canadian author Nalo Hopkinson's *The Chaos*, with a mixed-race protagonist, speculative setting, and explicit discussion of race, sexuality, and disability, is centered in the genre of contemporary adolescent fiction. As the novel begins, Scotch, who had to leave her old school because she was bullied so badly, and her brother Richard, whose parents called the police on him for smoking a joint, are planning to move out. It would be easy to read this novel as simply reinforcing the story of parent/teen conflict. But as the world of contemporary Toronto starts to fall apart, and Baba Yaga's house flies through the air, Richard apologizes because he didn't take Scotch seriously when she tried to get his help: "I thought you were just being a girl. You know, all whiny and shit." Scotch replies, "I was just a big ball of mad at everybody, and scared." Richard's answer, "Yeah, welcome to being a teenager," builds on an assumption that alienation and fear are simply the conditions of puberty (203).

What is actually crazy about Scotch's world—even before a volcano appears in the middle of Lake Ontario and her skin is covered in an asphalt-like substance—is that she was bullied to the point of violence at her old school. And her happiness at her new high school, from the perspective of a Backfisch narrative, is that now she does have someone—her friend Ben—who tells her what the rules are and gives her strategies for succeeding. The chaos that appears in Toronto, like the chaos of Scotch's school experience, makes no sense, is painful, and leaves Scotch feeling very much alone. When the world falls apart, Scotch learns Ben is not the only one she can turn to. Scotch can call for help and be answered, even if help comes in the form of an "old witch" with a flying house who threatens to make Scotch her maid. As "Horseless Head Men" appear and Ben discovers a creature who "smile[s] like lemon drops" (136), he tells Scotch, "We make the world a crazy place. Maybe some of it is that our crazy isn't invisible anymore" (137). In this novel, Scotch can let go of her relentless work to be the perfect girl, and she finds she is loved anyway.

These three contemporary novels for adolescent girls first portray their protagonists struggling to grow in unsympathetic environments before recognizing the girls' despair and alienation as a symptom of their need for nurture. Perhaps because Backfisch books do not engage in explicit cultural critique, it is easy to see them as agents of a conservative domestic ideology that restricts the lives of young women. These novels also give us powerful images of adolescence as a transformative space.

Contemporary scholarship on adolescence tends to focus on the adolescent as a problem—for herself and for her community. She is a mysterious figure, at odds with the adults in her life, unhappy, at risk. The Backfisch story can help us to understand this category that continues to engage and perplex us. The adolescent reminds us of our past—childhood—and anticipates our future—an evolving adulthood. She speaks to that part of ourselves that continues to be in flux. What does it mean that we are sometimes logical, sometimes emotional, sometimes both at once? How do we deal with the fact that we continually make mistakes, mislead others, have our feelings hurt? The messiness of adolescence is not a stage to be outgrown, but one we carry with us, long after the hormones of puberty have done their work. Understanding adolescence not only helps us to explain the behavior of teenagers, it also helps us construct structures that support us when our own lives no longer fit us. The orphan girl novel suggests we must escape abusive situations and earn the love of our communities to be happy. The Backfisch novel, on the other hand, tells us we are safe, and that our need to change is a mark of human growth, not sin. The awkward, cherished adolescent girl—so popular in mid-nineteenth-century fiction for girls—may have receded from the best-seller lists, but she remains a valuable resource for understanding contemporary girls and stories about them.

Notes

Unless otherwise noted, translations are the author's.

Introduction

1. See Estes and Lant, "Dismembering the Text."
2. Early definitions of the genre appear in Judith Rowbatham's *Good Girls Make Good Wives* (1989); Kimberley Reynolds's *Girls Only? Gender and Popular Juvenile Fiction in Britain, 1880–1910* (1990); Gillian Avery's *Behold the Child: American Children and Their Books 1621–1922* (1994); Anne Scott MacLeod's *American Childhood: Essays on Children's Literature of the Nineteenth and Twentieth Centuries* (1994); Foster and Simons's *What Katy Read* (1995); Lynne Vallone's *Disciplines of Virtue: Girls' Culture in the Eighteenth and Nineteenth Centuries* (1995); and Sally Mitchell's *The New Girl: Girls' Culture in England, 1880–1915* (1995).

More recent discussions include John Seelye's *Jane Eyre's American Daughters* (2005); Joe Sutliff Sanders's *Disciplining Girls: Understanding the Origins of the Classic Orphan Girl Story* (2011); Emily Hamilton-Honey's *Turning the Pages of American Girlhood: The Evolution of Girls' Series Fiction, 1865–1930* (2013); Beth Rodgers's *Adolescent Girlhood and Literary Culture at the Fin de Siècle: Daughters of Today* (2016); Nazera Sadiq Wright's *Black Girlhood in the Nineteenth Century* (2016); and Michelle J. Smith, Kristine Moruzi, and Clare Bradford's *From Colonial to Modern: Transnational Girlhood in Canadian, Australian, and New Zealand Literature, 1840–1940* (2018).

3. For more about the juvenile audience. See Foster and Simons, *What Katy Read*, 8–13.
4. Sarah Wadsworth provides a thoughtful overview of the conditions that led to "a formal separation of adult and juvenile readership" (17).
5. For a discussion of access to literacy for American girls, see Jane Greer, ed., *Girls and Literacy in America: Historical Perspectives to the Present* (2003) and Wright, *Black Girlhood*.

6. An abridgement of Richardson's novels was published in English as *The Paths of Virtue Delineated, or, the History in Miniature of the Celebrated Pamela, Clarissa Harlow, and Sir Charles Grandison, Familiarized and Adapted to the Capacities of Youth* (1756) and in German as *Die Wege der Tugend, oder die Geschichte der Pamela der berühmten Clarissa Harlowe und der Ritter Karl Grandisons im Kleinen entworfen* (1765).

7. Though these novels were addressed to the girl reader, girls' books were certainly read by men as well as girls and women. See Rob Hardy's "The Male Readers of *Rebecca of Sunnybrook Farm*."

8. Wright provides a substantial discussion of the work of Black authors for Black girls; Vanessa Steinroetter discusses the ways that reading provided Black women and girls with a path to increased social status.

9. Avery, *Behold the Child*; Nodelman, "Progressive Utopia"; Sanders, *Disciplining Girls*.

10. See Todd Kontje, *Women, the Novel, and the German Nation 1771–1871*.

11. The German film is titled *So Einfach ist die Liebe nicht* and premiered in Germany in 1949.

12. See Sarah Day, *Reading Like a Girl*, for a discussion of this theme in contemporary girls' books.

13. See Askey's *Good Girls, Good Germans* for further discussion of this point. Askey argues that "writing for the middle-class girls they themselves once were, these authors model a conservative, patriarchally oriented femininity that simultaneously attempts to locate moments of agency and power within existing social structures and expectations" (11). Similarly, Daniela Richter, in *Domesticating the Public: Women's Discourse on Gender Roles in Nineteenth-Century Germany*, claims that women's fiction is less conservative than other critics have asserted and that it does have feminist and emancipatory potential (14).

14. In *Comparative Children's Literature*, Emer O'Sullivan looks to the family story *Little Women* as the model nineteenth-century American girls' book and concludes that because German girls' books of the period focus on "tales of individual development," they "appear more progressive than the American family story" (43). Similarly, in his study of the sentimental origins of American girls' fiction, Sanders describes Johanna Spyri's best-selling *Heidi* as unlike the classic novels that are his focus. There are two exceptions, focusing on later girls' books. Nodelman, who argues against national difference in the girls' book, writes that heroines of the traditional novel for girls "all live the same story, and ... come to seem like variations of an ideal of female childhood that transcends national boundaries." Nodelman focuses on orphan girl novels that feature a protagonist of "five or nine but ... most likely eleven" (9). The loveable orphan whom he describes emerges later in the development of the genre of girls' fiction, but stories that celebrate adolescence also create cross-cultural connection. More recently, Jennifer Redmann's insightful essay, "Doing Her Bit: German and

Anglo-American Girls' Literature of the First World War" (2011), argues that "regardless of geographic location or national identity, common themes emerge in books written for middle-class adolescent girls during the war" (14).

15. For example, Barbara White claims that "our early novelists lack any conception of female adolescence," and "tend to ignore the years from eleven to sixteen or seventeen . . . as a period of little importance in itself or of little interest to the reader" (21).

16. As Christine Doyle points out, "The March trilogy abounds in favorable references to German culture in general and to German writers specifically" (50).

17. See Sanderson, *They Wrote for a Living*, for a full list of translations of *The Wide, Wide World*.

18. See Ochoa, "Protection for Works of Foreign Origin Under the 1909 Copyright Act."

19. In *Transnationalism and American Literature: Literary Translation 1773–1892*, Colleen Glenney Boggs points out that the current state of the publishing industry makes it difficult for us to comprehend the extent to which translated foreign texts dominated the nineteenth-century American publishing scene (31–32). See also *German Writing, American Reading: Women and the Import of Fiction, 1866–1917*, where Lynne Tatlock provides a fascinating look at "a German literature that seeped into American culture via popular reading in translation; it brought with it a host of beliefs and values that reinforced and sometimes expanded the boundaries of American domesticity" (5).

20. While the girls' book is also an important genre in England in the mid-nineteenth century, I've not been able to identify examples of Backfisch novels written by British authors. In other countries the girls' book emerges later, closer to the end of the nineteenth century. For discussions of colonial girlhood, see Kristine Moruzi and Michelle J. Smith, *Colonial Girlhood in Literature, Culture and History, 1840–1950* and Smith, Moruzi, and Bradford, *From Colonial to Modern*.

21. For a fascinating discussion of female puberty, see Hellen King, *The Disease of Virgins: Green Sickness, Chlorosis and the Problems of Puberty*, especially pp. 72–73.

22. Much has been written about the differences in feminist movements and the education of girls in the United States and Germany. For an early source, see Kasuya, *A Comparative Study of the Secondary Education of Girls in England, Germany, and the United States with a Consideration of the Secondary Education of Girls in Japan* (1933). More recent sources include Weedon, *Gender, Feminism, & Fiction in Germany, 1840–1914*. Weedon points to the difference between "the egalitarian model of emancipation," which was evident in the United States and Britain, and the "dualist model, dominant in Germany, which conceived of men and women as different but complementary" (13). See also Richter's *Domesticating the Public* for a useful overview of the social conditions and literary texts that

shaped conversations around gender in nineteenth-century Germany. Richter points out that Germany was later than the United States and Great Britain to engage in public debates about women's education (61).

23. In 1815 the Congress of Vienna created the German confederation, a collection of thirty-nine states intended to replace the structure of the Holy Roman Empire, which ceased to exist with the abdication of Francis II. Leadership of the confederation was held in Vienna, and the goal of the confederation was loose government for mutual protection, not a unified national identity. Prussia's desire for more power destabilized the confederation, and it was finally dissolved in 1866 after the Seven Weeks War. In 1871, when a number of southern German states joined the North German confederation, the German empire was named, and what is now modern Germany began the work of constructing itself as a unified nation-state.

24. Eugenie Marlitt's *Das Heideprinzesschen* (1871) was first published in serial form in *Die Gartenlaube: Illustriertes Familienblatt* (*The Garden Arbor: Illustrated Family Journal*) and then as a novel. The novel was translated by Mrs. A. L. Wister as *The Little Moorland Princess* and again by an anonymous translator as *The Princess of the Moor*. In an 1897 *Catalogue of A Very Fine Collection of Books, Das Haideprinceschen* is described as "The *vade-mecum* of the German 'Backfisch'" (67).

25. "Susan Coolidge" was a pen name for Sarah Chauncey Woolsey.

26. Translated by Marie Morgenstern as *Die Perle der Familie: Eine Erzählung aus dem häuslichen Leben*. The novel was also translated into Dutch, Norwegian, and French; it went through at least thirty-five editions between 1853 and 1915 and was reissued as recently as 1999.

27. *An Old-Fashioned Girl* is translated as *Ein Mädchen aus der guten alten Schule* (1872, 1873, 1883, 1898).

28. Spyri's title explicitly references Goethe's foundational Bildungsromane *Wilhelm Meisters Lehrjahre* (1796) and *Wilhelm Meisters Wanderjahre* (1821, 1829), with the title *Heidis Lehr- und Wanderjahre* (1880).

29. For a full list of translated editions of *Heidi*, see O'Sullivan, "The Little Swiss Girl from the Mountains: *Heidi* in Englischen Übersetzungen," and Susan Stan, "*Heidi* in English: A Bibliographic Study."

Chapter 1: Defining the Backfisch

1. Hall was not alone in his interest in the female adolescent. Starting in the nineteenth century, as Crista DeLuzio persuasively argues in her book, *Female Adolescence in American Scientific Thought, 1830–1930*, scientists in a variety of fields became engrossed by the question of child development. There are multiple explanations for a new focus on the adolescent girl in the Victorian era. Sarah Bilston suggests that the image of the eighteen-year-old Victoria transforming

overnight into a queen in 1837 drew attention to the movement from girl to woman; in an age of revolution, the idea of individual rebellion became particularly intriguing; at the same time, in reaction to free-thinking ideas of the 1840s and increased opportunities for individual choice, concerns about the proper education of young women moved to the forefront. In *Rites of Passage: Adolescence in America 1790 to the Present*, Joseph Kett points to industrialization as a cause for cultural shift—the movement of youth from agrarian work to the cities led to increased independence for young people and increased concern about how to maintain control over their behavior.

2. See Trites, *Twain, Alcott, and the Birth of the Adolescent Reform Novel*, for a discussion of adolescence as a literary topic in the nineteenth century and Foster and Simons, *What Katy Read*, for an insightful overview of the fictional representation of girlhood in this period.

3. I draw here on Todd Kontje's insightful comments on the Bildungsroman: "Female independence and potential for growth occur only in the brief period between leaving home and entering into marriage" (40). This is exactly the period on which the Backfisch novel focuses. See *Women, the Novel, and the German Nation 1771–1871*.

4. Though read by girls, the original German publication would have been aimed at adult readers; a later adaptation was abridged for a younger audience. See Eugenie Marlitt, *Heideprinzeßchen*, ed. Marie Otto.

5. While such family-oriented books have prompted Emer O'Sullivan to see German girls' novels of "individual development" as standing in contrast to American and British family stories of the same period, there are clearly early girls' novels in the United States that are actually in a similar vein. For more discussion of this point, see O'Sullivan's *Comparative Children's Literature*, 43.

6. In the first section, Polly looks like the classic heroine whom Nodelman describes in "Progressive Utopia: Or, How to Grow Up Without Growing Up."

Chapter 2: The Romance of Othermothering

1. This chapter examines four novels: the American *The Flower of the Family* (1853; translated *Die Perle der Familie*, 1875) and *Faith Gartney's Girlhood* (1863; translated *Faith Gartney's Mädchenjahre*, 1878) as well as the German *Backfischen's Leiden und Freuden* (1863; translated *Gretchen's Joys and Sorrows*, 1877) and *Der Trotzkopf* (1885; translated both *An Obstinate Maid* and *Taming a Tomboy*, 1898).

2. Patricia Hill Collins takes the word "othermother" from the work of Rosalie Riegle Troester.

3. I am indebted to Joel Clark, Roger McCoy, and Pamela J. Keller, who explain, "We can think of adolescent fiction about adolescent girls as a way in which women authors 'othermother' adolescent readers with stories about crises that other adolescents, their central characters, have experienced" (225).

4. In this, the girls' book follows a wider pattern in the novel. For more on this shift, see Lubovich, "'Married or Single?'" and Berend, "'The Best or None!'"

5. See, for example, MacLeod, "American Girlhood in the Nineteenth Century: Caddie Woodlawn's Sisters," in *American Childhood: Essays on Children's Literature in the Nineteenth and Twentieth Centuries*.

6. *Der Trotzkopf* was translated twice in 1898. I use the more skillful of the two translations, Mary Ireland's *An Obstinate Maid*, as well as my own translation of the German.

Chapter 3: Converting Girls into Women

1. An English-language edition of *The Wide, Wide World* was published in Germany in 1854 (Leipzig: Bernhard Tauchnitz). The novel was first published in German in 1853 as *Die Weite, Weite Welt*; multiple German-language editions followed, often with the added subtitle "a narrative for female youth." For more information, see Sanderson, *They Wrote for a Living*.

2. Like Butler, West and Zimmerman draw our attention to the ways that individual actions construct gender identity, but as Risman and Davis point out, while Butler sees the self as an "imaginary figment," West and Zimmerman rely on a notion of stable self that exists outside of gender performance.

3. See Grenz, *Mädchenliteratur im 18. und frühen 19. Jahrhunderst* (Girls' Literature of the 18th and Early 19th Centuries). Grenz goes on to argue: "This leads to the reader's guilt—it is possible to do this; when I'm not happy it's my own fault. It ignores the hard work that is necessary to call into question social norms, patterns of behavior, the realization that the reality of dominant ideologies, and one's acceptance of them, hinders the satisfaction of individual needs" (218, my translation).

4. In looking to the etymology of the word *Bildung*, Todd Kontje explains that "pietists conceived of *Bildung* as God's active transformation of the passive Christian" (1). For more about how *Bildung* represents the impression of God's image on the believer, see Bennett.

5. My translation. The original passage reads as follows: "So würde ich denn auch innerlich noch gehobelt und poliert, und Geist und Körper um die Wette in die höhere Schule geschickt" (chapter 4).

6. Others have pointed out that the domestic novel and adolescent girls' book highlight the work required of girls and women. Claudia Nelson argues in her essay "Domestic" in *Keywords for Children's Literature* that "the energy of the domestic novel for children derives" from "the recognition that achieving and maintaining what is domestic, whether defined as intimacy, familiarity, or housewifery, is often neither easy nor pleasant" (70).

Chapter 4: The Backfisch and the Fantasies of Growth

1. See Levander and her discussion of the ways that "novels teach readers to desire—and illustrate how they might acquire—whiteness, regardless of their racial identity, as a signature trait of national incorporation and affiliation" (90).

Chapter 5: The Homesick Heroine

1. Maria Nikolajeva helps us see this tension in her essay, "Tamed Imagination: A Re-reading of Heidi," where she points to the contradiction "between adults' almost compulsory need to socialize children and adults' nostalgic idealization of childhood as innocent and blissful" (68).

2. It is interesting that most English translations of *Heidis Lehr- und Wanderjahr* shorten the title to simply *Heidi*. This revision erases the link to high culture and the Bildungsroman that Spyri accomplishes by suggesting that Heidi's story is linked to the foundational Bildungsroman (Goethe, *Wilhelm Meisters Lehrjahre* [1796] and *Wilhelm Meisters Wanderjahre* [1821, 1829]).

3. See Leo Schelbert, *Historical Dictionary of Switzerland*.

4. See Stan, "*Heidi* in English."

5. In her essay "Between Hysteria and 'Heimweh': Heidi's Homesickness," Annie Pfeifer considers Heidi's homesickness as a gendered disease and as the expression of repressed childhood trauma.

6. See Karl Jaspers's 1909 Heidelberg medical thesis, cited in Ingrid Bauer's thesis, "Living in an Unidyllic Idyll: The Worlds of Anne and Heidi."

Works Cited

Primary Sources

Alcott, Louisa May. "Happy Women." In *Alternative Alcott*. Edited by Elaine Showalter. New Brunswick, NJ: Rutgers University Press, 1995.

Alcott, Louisa May. *Little Women, or, Meg, Jo, Beth And Amy*. Boston: Roberts Brothers, 1869. Hathi Trust. https://babel.hathitrust.org/cgi/pt?id=nc01.ark:/13960/t5z61j613&view=1up&seq=9.

Alcott, Louisa May. *Ein Mädchen aus der guten alten Schule*. Translated by Mary C. Rothwell. Stuttgart: Nitzschke, 1872.

Alcott, Louisa May. *An Old-Fashioned Girl*. Boston: Roberts Brothers, 1870. Hathi Trust. https://catalog.hathitrust.org/Record/001421444.

Alcott, Louisa May. *An Old-Fashioned Girl*. Leipzig: Bernhard Tauchnitz, 1883. Hathi Trust. https://catalog.hathitrust.org/Record/012372501.

Bismarck, Otto von. "Blut und Eisen." September 1862. Deutsche Geschichte in Dokumenten und Bildern. http://ghdi.ghi-dc.org/sub_document.cfm?document_id=250&language=german.

Bodewig, Paula. "Letters to Susan Warner." 24 January 1882 and 18 October 1882. Constitution Island Association. drive.google.com/file/d/0B1cre7-2DmIhbUJGNWgzZ1VfVok/view.

Browning, Robert. "Pippa's Song." Poetry. N.d. www.poetry.net/poem/30402/pippa's-song.

Burnett, Frances Hodgson. *The Secret Garden*. New York, Frederick Stokes, 1911.

Campe, Joachim Heinrich. *Väterlicher Rath für meine Tochter*. Braunschweig: Verlag der Schulbuchhandlung, 1796.

Canfield, Dorothy. *Understood Betsy*. New York: Henry Holt, 1917. Project Gutenberg. https://www.gutenberg.org/files/5347/5347-h/5347-h.htm. First published 1916.

Coolidge, Susan. *Wenn Morgen Heute Ist*. Translated by Erna Meyer-Voigt. Berlin: Erich Schmidt Verlag, 1956.

Coolidge, Susan. *What Katy Did*. Boston: Roberts Brothers, 1887. http://www.digital.library.upenn.edu/women/coolidge/katy/katy.html. First published 1872.

Coolidge, Susan. *What Katy Did at School*. 1873. Project Gutenberg. www.gutenberg.org/files/5141/5141.txt.

Darwin, C. R. *Über die Entstehung der Arten im Thier- und Pflanzen-Reich durch natürliche Züchtung, oder, Erhaltung der vervollkommneten Rassen im Kampfe um's Daseyn*. Translated by H. G. Bronn. Stuttgart: E. Schweizerbart'sche Verlagshandlung, 1860.

Fielding, Sarah. *The Governess: Or, The Little Female Academy*. London, 1749. Project Gutenberg. www.gutenberg.org/files/1905/1905-h/1905-h.htm.

Fielding, Sarah. *Die Hofmeisterinn, oder die kleine Akademie für das Frauenzimmer: zum Vergnügen und Unterrichte junger Personen dieses Geschlechtes bei ihrer Erziehung*. Leipzig, 1761.

Goethe, Johann Wolfgang. *Wilhelm Meisters Lehrjahre. Ein Roman*. Berlin: Johann Friedrich Unger, 1795–1796.

Hamilton, Virginia. *Sweet Whispers, Brother Rush*. New York: Harper Collins, 2001. First published 1982.

Helm, Clementine. *Backfischen's Leiden und Freuden: Eine Geschichte für junge Mädchen*. Leipzig, 1882. Project Gutenberg. www.gutenberg.org/files/48064/48064-h/48064-h.htm. First published 1863.

Helm, Clementine. *Gretchen's Joys and Sorrows*. Translated by Helen Dunbar Slack. Boston: A. Williams, 1877. Internet Archive. archive.org/details/gretchensjoysanoobeyrgoog/page/n24.

Helm, Clementine. *A Miss in Her Teens: A Tale for Girls*. Translated by Rhoda E. Colborne. London: J. W. Kolckmann, 1877. Internet Archive. archive.org/stream/amissinherteensoohelmgoog/amissinherteensoohelmgoog_djvu.txt.

Hopkinson, Nalo. *The Chaos*. New York: Simon and Schuster, 2012.

Keyssler, Johann. *Travels through Germany*. London, 1758.

Lincoln, Abraham. "The Gettysburg Address." 19 November 1863. www.ushistory.org/documents/gettysburg.htm.

Marlitt, Eugenie. *Das Heideprinzeßchen*. Leipzig, 1871. Hathi Trust. babel.hathitrust.org/cgi/pt?id=umn.319510020850533&view=1up&seq=7.

Marlitt, Eugenie. *Heideprinzeßchen*. Abridged by Marie Otto. Berlin: Meidinger's Jugendschriften Verlag, 1889.

Marlitt, Eugenie. *The Little Moorland Princess*. Translated by Mrs. A. L. Wister. Philadelphia: Lippincott, 1872. Hathi Trust. babel.hathitrust.org/cgi/pt?id=hvd.32044087192860&view=1up&seq=9.

Marlitt, Eugenie. *The Little Princess*. Translated by Blanche E. Slade. London: Remington, 1883. Internet Archive. archive.org/details/littleprincessfoojohngoog/page/n5.

Marlitt, Eugenie. *The Princess of the Moor*. New York: A. L. Burt, 1890. Hathi Trust. babel.hathitrust.org/cgi/pt?id=uc2.ark:/13960/t8bg2kd03&view=1up&seq=5.

McCall, Guadalupe Garcia. *Under the Mesquite*. New York: Lee and Low, 2011.

Milton, John. *Paradise Lost*. London: Samuel Simmons, 1674.

Montgomery, L. M. *Anne of Green Gables*. 1908. Project Gutenberg. www.guten berg.org/files/45/45-h/45-h.htm.
Porter, Eleanor. *Pollyanna*. Boston: L. C. Page and Company, 1913.
Prentiss, Elizabeth. *The Flower of the Family: A Book for Girls*. New York: A. D. F. Randolph, 1883. Internet Archive. archive.org/details/flowerfamilyabooopren goog/page/n170. First published 1853.
Prentiss, Elizabeth. *Die Perle der Familie*. Translated by Marie Morgenstern. Basil, 1875.
Prentiss, Elizabeth. *Stepping Heavenward*. New York: Anson D. F. Randolph, 1869.
Richardson, Samuel. *The Paths of Virtue Delineated, or, the History in Miniature of the Celebrated Pamela, Clarissa Harlow, and Sir Charles Grandison, Familiarized and Adapted to the Capacities of Youth*. London, 1756.
Richardson, Samuel. *Die Wege der Tugend, oder die Geschichte der Pamela der berühmten Clarissa Harlowe und der Ritter Karl Grandisons im Kleinen entworfen*. Altenburg, 1765.
Schmidt, Fr. "Evolution of Household Articles, Animals etc. According to Darwin's Doctrine." [1860–1869?]. Color lithographs. Wellcome Library, London. wellcomelibrary.org/item/b16804065#?c=0&m=0&s=0&cv=0&z=-0.6479 %2C-0.072%2C2.2957%2C1.4401.
Sidgwick, Mrs. Alfred. *Home Life in Germany*. New York: Chautauqua Press, 1908.
Spyri, Johanna. *Heidi: Her Years of Wandering and Learning. A Story for Children and Those Who Love Children*. Translated by Louise Brooks. New York: Platt and Peck, 1884. Hathi Trust. hdl.handle.net/2027/uc2.ark:/13960/t7hq43s72.
Spyri, Johanna. *Heidi: How She Used What She Learned. A Story for Children and Those Who Love Children*. Translated by Louise Brooks. Boston, 1885. First published 1884.
Spyri, Johanna. *Heidi Kann Brauchen, Was Es Gelernt Hat*. Gotha: Friedrich Perthes, 1881. Hathi Trust. https://catalog.hathitrust.org/Record/100532147.
Spyri, Johanna. *Heidis Lehr- und Wanderjahre*. Gotha: Friedrich Perthes, 1880. Project Gutenberg. www.gutenberg.org/files/7500/7500-h/7500-h.htm.
Ullrich, Hortense. *Hexen Küsst man nicht*. Stuttgart: Thienemann Verlag, 1999.
Von Rhoden, Emmy. *An Obstinate Maid*. Translated by Mary E. Ireland. Philadelphia: George W. Jacobs, 1898.
Von Rhoden, Emmy. *Taming a Tomboy*. Translated from the 25th edition by Felix Oswald. New York, 1898. Internet Archive. archive.org/details/tamingtomboy 00rhod/page/n8.
Von Rhoden, Emmy. *Der Trotzkopf. Eine Pensionsgeschichte für junge Mädchen*. Stuttgart, Germany: Verlag von Gustav Weise, 1885. Internet Archive. archive .org/stream/dertrotzkopf31309gut/31309-pdf_djvu.txt.
Warner, Susan. Letter to Paula Bodewig. [1882?]. Constitution Island Association. drive.google.com/file/d/0B1cre7-2DmIhbUJGNWgzZ1VfVok/view.
Warner, Susan. *Die Weite, Weite Welt: Aus dem Englischen*. Translated by Dr. J. Biethen. Leipzig, 1853. Internet Archive. https://archive.org/details/bub_gb _bKpMAAAAcAAJ/page/n1/mode/2up.

Warner, Susan. *The Wide, Wide World*. New York: Grosset and Dunlap, 1853. Project Gutenberg. http://www.gutenberg.org/files/28376/28376-h/28376-h.htm. First published 1850.

Whitney, Mrs. A. D. T. *Faith Gartney's Girlhood*. Boston: Houghton Mifflin, 1892. First published 1863.

Whitney, Mrs. A. D. T. *Faith Gartney's Mädchenjahre*. Translated by P. E. B. Leipzig: Adolph Russell, 1878.

Wiggin, Kate Douglass. *Rebecca of Sunnybrook Farm*. Boston: Houghton Mifflin Harcourt, 1903.

Wordsworth, William. "Ode: Intimations of Immortality from Recollections of Early Childhood." 1807. www.poetryfoundation.org/poems/45536/ode-intimations-of-immortality-from-recollections-of-early-childhood.

Secondary Sources

Acker, Joan. "From Sex Roles to Gendered Institutions." *Contemporary Sociology* 21, no. 5 (1992): 565–69.

Allen, Ann Taylor. *Feminism and Motherhood in Germany, 1800–1914*. New Brunswick, NJ: Rutgers University Press, 1991.

Alves, Jaime Osterman. *Fictions of Female Education in the Nineteenth Century*. New York: Routledge, 2009.

Anderson, Benedict. *Imagined Communities: Reflections on the Origin and Spread of Nationalism*. New York: Verso, 1991.

Askey, Jennifer Drake. *Good Girls, Good Germans: Girls' Education and Emotional Nationalism in Wilhelminian Germany*. Rochester, NY: Camden House, 2013.

Attebery, Brian. "Elizabeth Enright and the Family Story as Genre." *Children's Literature* 37 (2009): 114–36.

Avery, Gillian. *Behold the Child: American Children and Their Books 1621–1922*. Baltimore: Johns Hopkins University Press, 1994.

"backfisch, n." *OED Online*. Oxford University Press, June 2019. Accessed 8 July 2019. www.oed.com/view/Entry/14390.

Bauer, Ingrid. "Living in an Unidyllic Idyll: The Worlds of Anne and Heidi: A Comparison between Johanna Spyri's Heidi and L. M. Montgomery's Anne of Green Gables." Master's thesis, McGill University, 2002. https://escholarship.mcgill.ca/concern/theses/d217qq181.

Baxter, Kent. *The Modern Age: Turn-of-the-Century American Culture and the Invention of Adolescence*. Tuscaloosa: University of Alabama Press, 2008.

Baym, Nina. *Women's Fiction*. Champaign: University of Illinois Press, 1993.

Bennett, Kelsey. *Principle and Propensity: Experience and Religion in the Nineteenth-Century British and American Bildungsroman*. Columbia: University of South Carolina Press, 2014.

Beran, Michael Know. *Forge of Empires: Three Revolutionary Statesmen and the World They Made, 1861–1871*. New York: Free Press, 2007.

Berend, Zsuzsa. "'The Best or None!' Spinsterhood in Nineteenth-Century New England." *Journal of Social History* 33, no. 4 (Summer 2000): 935–57.

Bernstein, Robin. "Childhood as Performance." In *The Children's Table: Childhood Studies and the Humanities*. Edited by Anna Mae Duane. Athens: University of Georgia Press, 2013, 203–12.

Bernstein, Robin. Introduction. *Racial Innocence: Performing American Childhood from Slavery to Civil Rights*. New York: New York University Press, 2011.

"Beyond the Borderline." *The Lancet Psychiatry* 6, no. 3 (1 March 2019). https://doi.org/10.1016/s2215-0366(19)30051-3.

Bilston, Sarah. *The Awkward Age in Women's Popular Fiction, 1850–1900*. New York: Oxford University Press, 2004.

Blamires, David. *Telling Tales: The Impact of Germany on English Children's Books: 1780–1918*. Cambridge, UK: Open Book Publishers, 2009.

Boggs, Colleen Glenney. *Transnationalism and American Literature: Literary Translation 1773–1892*. New York: Routledge, 2007.

Butler, Judith. *Undoing Gender*. New York: Routledge, 2004.

Capshaw, Katharine, and Anna Mae Duane, eds. *Who Writes for Black Children? African American Children's Literature before 1900*. Minneapolis: University of Minnesota Press, 2017.

Chodorow, Nancy. *The Reproduction of Mothering: Psychoanalysis and the Sociology of Gender*. Berkeley: University of California Press, 1978.

Clark, Roger, Joel McCoy, and Pamela J. Keller. "Teach Your Children Well: Reading Lessons to and about Black and White Adolescent Girls from Black and White Women Authors." *International Review of Modern Sociology* 34, no. 2 (Autumn 2008): 211–28.

Collins, Patricia Hill. *Black Feminist Thought: Knowledge, Consciousness, and the Politics of Empowerment*. New York: Routledge, 1991.

Collins, Patricia Hill. "Shifting the Center: Race, Class, and Feminist Theorizing About Motherhood." In *Mothering: Ideology, Experience, and Agency*, edited by Evelyn Nakano Glenn, Grace Chang, and Linda Rennie Forcey. New York: Routledge, 1994.

Collins, Patricia Hill. "Toward a New Vision: Race, Class, and Gender as Categories of Analysis and Connection." *Race, Gender, and Class* 1, no. 1 (Fall 1993): 25–45.

Cramer, Lloyd. *Nationalism in Europe and America: Politics, Cultures, and Identities Since 1775*. Chapel Hill: University of North Carolina Press, 2011.

Davis, Lennard J. *Bending Over Backwards: Disability, Dismodernism, and Other Difficult Positions*. New York: New York University Press, 2002.

Day, Sarah. *Reading Like a Girl: Narrative Intimacy in Contemporary American Young Adult Literature*. Jackson: University Press of Mississippi, 2015.

DeLuzio, Crista. *Female Adolescence in American Scientific Thought, 1830–1930*. Baltimore: Johns Hopkins University Press, 2007.

DiQuinzio, Patrice. *The Impossibility of Motherhood: Feminism, Individualism, and the Problem of Mothering*. New York: Routledge, 1999.

Doyle, Christine. "Singing Mignon's Song: German Literature and Culture in the March Trilogy." *Children's Literature* 31 (2003): 50–70.

Duane, Anna Mae. *The Children's Table: Childhood Studies and The Humanities*. Athens: University of Georgia Press, 2013.

Duane, Anna Mae. *Suffering Childhood in Early America: Violence, Race, and the Making of the Child Victim*. Athens: University of Georgia Press, 2010.

"During World War I, U.S. Government Propaganda Erased German Culture." National Public Radio, 7 April 2017. https://www.npr.org/2017/04/07/523044253/during-world-war-i-u-s-government-propaganda-erased-german-culture.

Ehrenpreis, David. "The Figure of the Backfisch: Representing Puberty in Wilhelmine Germany." *Zeitschrift fur Kunstgeschichte* 67, no. 4 (2004): 479–508.

Eigler, Friederike, and Susane Kord, editors. *The Feminist Encyclopedia of German Literature*. Westport, CT: Greenwood Press, 1997.

Estes, Angela M., and Kathleen Margaret Lant. "Dismembering the Text: The Horror of Louisa May Alcott's *Little Women*." *Children's Literature* 17 (1989): 98–123.

Ferrall, Charles, and Anna Jackson. *Juvenile Literature and British Society, 1850–1950: The Age of Adolescence*. New York: Routledge, 2010.

Foster, Shirley, and Judy Simons. *What Katy Read: Feminist Re-Readings of 'Classic' Stories for Girls*. Iowa City: University of Iowa Press, 1995.

Giffen, Allison, and Robin L. Cadwallader. *Saving the World: Girlhood and Evangelicalism in Nineteenth-Century Literature*. New York: Routledge, 2018.

Glenn, Evelyn Nakano. "Social Constructions of Mothering: A Thematic Overview." In *Mothering: Ideology, Experience, and Agency*, edited by Evelyn Nakano Glenn, Grace Chang, and Linda Rennie Forcey. New York: Routledge, 1994.

Greer, Jane, editor. *Girls and Literacy in America: Historical Perspectives to the Present*. Santa Barabara, CA: ABC-CLIO, 2003.

Grenz, Dagmar. *Mädchenliteratur: Von den moralisch-belehrenden Schriften im 18. Jahrhundert bis zur Herausbildung der Backfischliteratur im 19. Jahrhundert*. Stuttgart: Metzlersche Verlagsbuchhandlung, 1981.

Grenz, Dagmar, and Gisela Wilkending. *Geschichte der Mädchenlektüre. Mädchenliteratur und die gesellschaftliche Situation der Frauen vom 18. Jahrhundert bis zur Gegenwart*. Weinheim/München: Juventa, 1997.

Gubar, Marah. *Artful Dodgers: Reconceiving the Golden Age of Children's Literature*. New York: Oxford University Press, 2009.

Gubar, Marah. "'Where is the Boy?': The Pleasures of Postponement in the Anne of Green Gables Series" *The Lion and the Unicorn* 25, no. 1 (January 2001): 47–69.

Hall, G. Stanley. *Adolescence, Its Psychology and Its Relations to Physiology, Anthropology, Sociology, Sex, Crime, Religion and Education*, 2 vols. New York: Appleton Press, 1904.

Hall, G. Stanley. "The Budding Girl." *Appleton's Magazine* 13 (January 1909): 47.
Hamilton-Honey, Emily. *Turning the Pages of American Girlhood: The Evolution of Girls' Series Fiction, 1865–1930.* Jefferson, NC: McFarland, 2013.
Hardy, Rob. "The Male Readers of *Rebecca of Sunnybrook Farm*." *The Lion and the Unicorn* 28, no. 1 (2004): 31–52. https://doi.org/10.1353/uni.2004.0004.
Harris, Susan K. "'But Is It Any Good?': Evaluating Nineteenth-Century American Women's Fiction." *American Literature* 63, no. 1 (1991): 43–61. www.jstor.org/stable/2926561.
Heaney, Howell J. "A Century of Early American Children's Books in German, 1738–1837." *Phaedrus: An International Journal of Children's Literature Research* 29, no. 1 (Spring 1979): 22–26.
"homesickness, n." *OED Online.* Oxford University Press, June 2019. Accessed 15 July 2019. www.oed.com/view/Entry/87934.
Hutcheon, Linda. "Irony, Nostalgia, and the Postmodern." In *Methods for the Study of Literature as Cultural Memory*, edited by Raymond Vervliet and Annemarie Estor. Rodopi: Atlanta, 2000.
Irving, Debbie. *Waking Up White and Finding Myself in the Story of Race.* Self-published, Elephant Room Press, 2014.
Kasuya, Yoshi. *A Comparative Study of the Secondary Education of Girls in England, Germany, and the United States.* New York: Teachers College, Columbia University, 1933.
Kett, Joseph F. *Rites of Passage: Adolescence in America 1790 to the Present.* New York: Basic Books, 1977.
King, Helen. *The Disease of Virgins: Green Sickness, Chlorosis and the Problems of Puberty.* New York: Routledge, 2009.
Kluge, Friedrich. *Etymologisches Wörterbuch der deutschen Sprache.* 18th ed. Edited by Walther Mitzka. Berlin: Walter de Gruyter, 1960. https://books.google.com/books?id=UGaEDwAAQBAJ&lpg=PA914&ots=-eBcsUStSp&dq=truebners%20deutsches%20worterbuch%20backfisch&pg=PR1#v=onepage&q&f=false.
Kontje, Todd. *Woman, the Novel, and the German Nation 1771–1871: Domestic Fiction in the Fatherland.* Cambridge, UK: Cambridge University Press, 1998.
Lerer, Seth. *Children's Literature.* Chicago: University of Chicago Press, 2008.
Levander, Caroline. *Cradle of Liberty: Race, the Child, and National Belonging from Thomas Jefferson to W. E. B. DuBois.* Durham, NC: Duke University Press, 2006.
Lubovich, Maglina. "'Married or Single?': Catharine Maria Sedgwick on Old Maids, Wives, and Marriage." *Legacy* 25, no. 1 (2008): 23–40.
MacLeod, Anne Scott. *American Childhood: Essays on Children's Literature in the Nineteenth and Twentieth Centuries.* Athens: University of Georgia Press, 1994.
Magyarody, Katherine. "Awkward and Awry: Novel Directions for Female Development in Charlotte Yonge's *The Daisy Chain*." *Nineteenth-Century Gender Studies* 14, no. 3 (2018).

Matt, Susan J. *Homesickness: An American History*. New York: Oxford University Press, 2011.

McQuillan, Julia, and Julie Pfeiffer. "Why Anne Makes Us Dizzy: Reading *Anne of Green Gables* from a Gender Perspective." *Mosaic: A Journal for the Interdisciplinary Study of Literature* (2001): 17–32.

Mitchell, Sally. *The New Girl: Girls' Culture in England, 1880–1915*. New York: Columbia University Press, 1995.

Moore, Cornelia Niekus. *The Maiden's Mirror: Reading Material for German Girls in the Sixteenth and Seventeenth Centuries*. Wiesbaden, Germany: Harrassowitz, 1987.

Moruzi, Kristine, and Michelle J. Smith. *Colonial Girlhood in Literature, Culture and History, 1840–1950*. London: Palgrave Macmillan, 2014.

Mott, Frank Luther. *Golden Multitudes*. New York: Macmillan, 1947.

Nelson, Claudia. "Domestic." In *Keywords for Children's Literature*, edited by Philip Nel and Lissa Paul, 67–70. New York: New York University Press, 2011.

Nikolajeva, Maria. "Tamed Imagination: A Re-reading of *Heidi*." *Children's Literature Association Quarterly* 25 no. 2 (Summer 2000): 68–75.

Nodelman, Perry. "Progressive Utopia: Or, How to Grow Up Without Growing Up." In *Such a Simple Little Tale: Critical Responses to L. M. Montgomery's "Anne of Green Gables,"* edited by Mavis Reimer, 30–45. Metuchen, NJ: Scarecrow Press, 1992.

"nostalgia, n." *OED Online*. Oxford University Press, June 2019. Accessed 15 July 2019. www.oed.com/view/Entry/128472.

Ochoa, Tyler T. "Protection for Works of Foreign Origin Under the 1909 Copyright Act." Santa Clara Law Digital Commons, 2010. digitalcommons.law.scu.edu/facpubs/53.

O'Sullivan, Emer. *Comparative Children's Literature*. New York: Routledge, 2005.

O'Sullivan, Emer. "The Little Swiss Girl from the Mountains: *Heidi* in Englischen Übersetzungen." In *Johanna Spyri und ihr Werk—Lesarten*, edited by Norbert Natros, 139–62. Zurich: Chronos Verlag, 2004.

Owen, Gabrielle. "Toward a Theory of Adolescence: Queer Disruptions in Representations of Adolescent Reading." *Jeunesse: Young People, Texts, Cultures* 7, no. 1 (2015): 110–34.

Pfeifer, Annie. "Between Hysteria and 'Heimweh': Heidi's Homesickness." *German Life and Letters* 72, no. 1 (January 2019): 52–63.

Pfeiffer, Julie. "The Backfisch and Stories of Female Adolescence." *Tulsa Studies in Women's Literature* 36, no. 2 (Fall 2017): 295–321.

Pfeiffer, Julie. "The Romance of Othermothering in Nineteenth-Century *Backfisch* Books." In *Mothers in Children's and Young Adult Literature*, edited by Lisa Rowe Fraustino and Karen Coats, 59–74. Jackson: University Press of Mississippi, 2016.

Quay, Sarah E. "Homesickness in Susan Warner's *The Wide, Wide World*." *Tulsa Studies in Women's Literature* 18 (Spring 1999): 39–58.

Redmann, Jennifer. "Doing Her Bit: German and Anglo-American Girls' Literature of the First World War." *Girlhood Studies* 4, no. 1 (Summer 2011): 10–29.

"Review of the Week." *American Publishers' Circular and Literary Gazette* 2, no. 26 (1856): 374.

Reynolds, Kimberley. *Girls Only? Gender and Popular Juvenile Fiction in Britain, 1880–1910*. Philadelphia: Temple University Press, 1990.

Richter, Daniela. *Domesticating the Public: Women's Discourse on Gender Roles in Nineteenth-Century Germany*. Oxford, UK: Peter Lang, 2012.

Rippley, La Vern J. "Conflict in the Classroom: Anti-Germanism in Minnesota Schools, 1917–19." *Minnesota History* (1981): 176.

Risman, Barbara. *Gender Vertigo*. New Haven, CT: Yale University Press, 1998.

Risman, Barbara, and Georgiann Davis. "From Sex Roles to Gender Structure." *Current Sociology* 61 no. 5–6 (2013): 733–55.

Robinson, Laura M. "'Sex Matters': L. M. Montgomery, Friendship, and Sexuality." *Children's Literature* 40 (2012): 167–90.

Rodgers, Beth. *Adolescent Girlhood and Literary Culture at the Fin de Siècle: Daughters of Today*. New York: Palgrave Macmillan, 2016.

Roth, Susan. *Report of the Duke University Women's Initiative*. 2003. university women.stanford.edu/reports/WomensInitiativeReport.pdf.

Rousseau, Jean-Jacques. *Émile: A Treatise on Education*. Translated by Barbara Foxley. https://archive.org/stream/in.ernet.dli.2015.226569/2015.226569 .Emile_djvu.txt.

Rowbatham, Judith. *Good Girls Make Good Wives: Guidance for Girls in Victorian Fiction*. Oxford, UK: Basil Blackwell, 1989.

Royster, Jacqueline Jones. *Traces of a Stream: Literacy and Social Change among African American Women*. Pittsburgh, PA: University of Pittsburgh Press, 2000.

Ryan, Mary P. *The Empire of the Mother: American Writing About Domesticity, 1830–1850*. New York: Routledge, 1982.

Sanders, Joe Sutliff. *Disciplining Girls: Understanding the Origins of the Classic Orphan Girl Story*. Baltimore: Johns Hopkins University Press, 2011.

Sanderson, Dorothy Hurlbut. *They Wrote for a Living: A Bibliography of the Works of Susan Bogert Warner and Anna Bartlett Warner*. Cold Spring, NY: Constitution Island Association, 1976.

Savage, Jon. *Teenage: The Creation of Youth Culture*. New York: Viking, 2007.

Schelbert, Leo. *Historical Dictionary of Switzerland*. Lanham, MD: Rowman and Littlefield, 2011.

Seelye, John. *Jane Eyre's American Daughters: From "The Wide, Wide World" to "Anne of Green Gables": A Study of Marginalized Maidens and What They Mean*. Newark: University of Delaware Press, 2005.

Skrine, Peter. "Johanna Spyri's *Heidi*." *Bulletin of the John Rylands University Library of Manchester* 76, no. 3 (1994): 145–64.

Smith, Michelle J., Kristine Moruzi, and Clare Bradford. *From Colonial to Modern: Transnational Girlhood in Canadian, Australian, and New Zealand Literature, 1840–1940*. Toronto, Canada: University of Toronto Press, 2018.

Smith-Rosenberg, Carroll. "The Female World of Love and Ritual: Relations between Women in Nineteenth-Century America." *Signs* 1, no. 1 (Autumn 1975): 1–29.

Stan, Susan. "*Heidi* in English: A Bibliographic Study." *New Review of Children's Literature and Librarianship* 16, no. 1 (2010): 1–23.

Steinroetter, Vanessa. "Daughters of a Reading People: Representations of African American Girlhood and Female Literacy in the Christian Recorder." In *Saving the World: Girlhood and Evangelicalism in Nineteenth-Century U.S. Literature*, edited by Robin Cadwallader and Allison Giffen, 52–70. London: Routledge, 2017.

Tatlock, Lynne. "Domesticated Romance and Capitalist Enterprise: Anis Lee Wister's Americanization of German Fiction." In *German Culture in Nineteenth-Century America: Reception, Adaptation, Transformation*, edited by Lynne Tatlock and Matt Erlin, 153–82. Rochester, NY: Camden House, 2005.

Tatlock, Lynne. "German Women Writers and the North American Market." In *German Writing, American Reading*, edited by Lynne Tatlock, 38–39. Columbus: Ohio State University Press, 2012.

Tatlock, Lynne. *German Writing, American Reading: Women and the Import of Fiction, 1866–1917*. Columbus: Ohio State University Press, 2012.

Tatlock, Lynne. *Publishing Culture and the "Reading Nation": German Book History in the Long Nineteenth Century*. Rochester, NY: Camden House, 2010.

Tompkins, Jane. *Sensational Designs: The Cultural Work of American Fiction, 1790–1869*. New York: Oxford University Press, 1986.

Trites, Roberta Seelinger. *Twain, Alcott, and the Birth of the Adolescent Reform Novel*. Iowa City: University of Iowa Press, 2007.

Troester, Rosalie Riegle. "Turbulence and Tenderness: Mothers, Daughters, and Othermothers in Paule Marshall's *Brown Girl, Brownstones*." *SAGE: A Scholarly Journal on Black Women* 1 (1984): 13–16.

Trubey, Elizabeth Fekete. "Imagined Revolution: The Female Reader and *The Wide, Wide World*." *Modern Language Studies* 31 (2001): 57–74.

Vallone, Lynne. *Disciples of Virtue: Girls' Culture in the Eighteenth and Nineteenth Centuries*. New Haven, CT: Yale University Press, 1995.

Vollmer, Clement. "The American Novel in Germany, 1871–1913." *German American Annals* 15, no. 19 (1917): 113–44, 165–219.

Wadsworth, Sarah. *In the Company of Books: Literature and Its "Classes" in Nineteenth-Century America*. University of Massachusetts Press, 2006.

Waller, Alison. *Constructing Adolescence in Fantastic Realism*. New York: Routledge, 2009.

Weedon, Chris. *Gender, Feminism, & Fiction in Germany, 1840–1014*. Oxford, UK: Peter Lang, 2006.

Weisbrode, Kenneth. "Why Bismarck Loved Lincoln." *New York Times*. 2 October 2011, https://opinionator.blogs.nytimes.com/2011/10/02/why-bismarck-loved-lincoln/.

West, Candace, and Don Zimmerman. "Doing Gender." *Gender and Society* 1, no. 2 (1987): 125–51.
Westwood, Thomas. *Catalogue of A Very Fine Collection of Books*. Piccadilly, London, 1897. Google Books. https://books.google.com/books?id=EDvhAAA AMAAJ&pg=PP9&lpg=PP9&dq=Westwood,+Thomas.+Catalogue+of+A+V ery+Fine+Collection+of+Books&source=bl&ots=o5LZwBHdJo&sig=ACfU3 U3eYfaQEVmy18WuDcWR6E-4SZf-MA&hl=en&sa=X&ved=2ahUKEwjwlf 3vooXuAhWizVkKHb5LB8oQ6AEwBnoECAcQAg#v=onepage&q=backfisc h&f=false.
White, Barbara. *Growing Up Female: Adolescent Girlhood in American Fiction*. Westport, CT: Greenwood Press, 1985.
Wilkending, Gisela. "Einleitung." In *Kinder und Jugendliteratur: Maedchenliteratur: Vom 18. Jahrhundert bis zum Zweiten Weltkrieg*. Stuttgart: Philipp Reclam, 1994.
Wilkending, Gisela. *Mädchenliterature der Kaiserzeit: Zwischen weiblicher Identifizierung und Grenzüberschreitung*. Stuttgart, Germany: J. B. Metzler, 2003.
Wright, Nazera Sadiq. *Black Girlhood in the Nineteenth Century*. Champaign: University of Illinois Press, 2016.
Yuval-Davis, Nira. *Gender & Nation*. London: SAGE Publications, 1997.
Zacharasiewicz, Waldemar. *Images of Germany in American Literature*. Iowa City: University of Iowa Press, 2007.

Index

adolescence: adult fears about, 23; alienation during, 23; Backfisch as descriptor of, 13–14, 18; as category of identity, 11, 24; contemporary views of, 22; critics on, 23–24, 174n1; development during, 93–116; as distinct developmental stage, 18; as flexible space of growth, 165–69; G. Stanley Hall on, 14, 19, 23–24, 24, 25, 42–43, 60, 64; growth and, 141–63; of liminal space, 45; longing for childhood in, 143; Margaret Mead on, 26; messiness of, 169; models of, 27; narratives of, 123–25; nationalism and, 119, 139; as natural period of identity development, 44; nineteenth-century views of, 22–23; as opportunity, 4; othermothering in, 66, 91; pain of, 127; as positive model, 38, 64, 139; as problem, 56; as time of self-transformation, 17, 75–76, 123, 168, 172n13; as time worth investment, 63–64

Adolescent Girlhood and Literary Culture at the Fin de Siecle: Daughters of Today (Rodgers), 24

Alcott, Louisa May, 32; European travels of, 19; "Happy Women," 71; *Little Women*, 4, 8, 19, 46, 53; *An Old-Fashioned Girl*, 27, 33–34, 44, 53, 56–60, 110; *The Wide, Wide World* and, 97

Allen, Ann Taylor, 119

Alves, Jaime Osterman, 18

American Childhood (MacLeod), 22, 120

Anne of Green Gables (Montgomery): female bonds in, 90; model of adolescence in, 41–42; model of womanhood in, 103; order in, 103; othermothering in, 74; shaping of community in, 9, 41; suffering in, 156; as tool for gender construction, 99–100

Anne Shirley (character): development in, 42; homesickness and, 152–53; as orphan girl, 152; self-control and, 152–54; shaping of community in, 9, 41. See also *Anne of Green Gables*

Askey, Jennifer Drake, 120, 123

Aunt Fortune (character), 73, 106, 108. See also *Wide, Wide World, The*

Aunt Ulrike (character): God-like role of, 76–77; love and, 46; as mentor, 76–77; as role model, 109–11, 121; as source of comfort, 106. See also *Backfischen's Leiden und Freuden*

Backfisch, the: and adolescence as space of growth, 165–66; adolescent girl as, 38, 43; allure and danger of, 60; characteristics of, 14–15, 38–39, 61; childhood and, 15; defining, 25, 41–64; etymology of, 13–14, 25; and fantasies of growth, 117–39; maturity as source of happiness and, 154; mentoring of, 74, 165; as metaphor for mid-nineteenth-century adolescent girl, 61–63; as model, 166; vs. the orphan girl, 152; othermothering and, 68–69, 87, 89–90; relationships among women and, 68; self-discovery and, 103; transformation of, 56; uses in English, 14

Backfisch book, 44; adult template in, 26; alternative model of adolescence in, 25–27; challenging of social norms in, 16–17; change as growth in, 169; characteristics of, 12, 14, 16; closure and, 103–5; community identity and, 122; contemporary adolescent literature and, 115; as conversion narrative, 114; as cookbook, 113; discomfort of change in, 126; examples of, 27–39; flexible growth in, 166; the "great social household" and, 119–23; healthy adolescence in, 91; homesickness in, 141–63; identifying adolescence, 24–25; invisible/visible labor in, 98; journey from home, 53; material vs. spiritual power in, 108; men in, 84; mother figures in, 66; narrator as mentor to readers in, 69–70; nationalism and, 118, 123; vs. orphan girl novel, 157; and the other, 138; othermothering in, 65–91; protagonist, healing of, 128; romance between women in, 65–66; social construction of womanhood in, 95, 115; storytelling in, 8, 67; successful growth in, 127; suffering in, 122–29; support of adults in, 115; teaching of domesticity in, 112; value of adolescence in, 144; white privilege in, 38, 133

Backfisch heroine: awkwardness of, 62; characteristics of, 15; cultural norms vs. choices, 53; "doing gender" and, 114; education of, 15; individual vs. community identity in, 121–22; journey from home of, 45; liminal space and, 61–62; mentoring and, 74, 154, 166; as model, 112–13; need for empathy and, 25; self-control and, 105, 148; self-discovery of, 103; self-transformation of, 30, 56, 62–63, 103; sexuality of, 46, 60–61; suffering and, 126; sympathetic portrayal of, 16

Backfischens Leiden und Freuden (Gretchen's Joys and Sorrows) (Helm), 27, 29, 95

Backfischliteratur. See Backfisch book

Backfischzeit (adolescent time): as challenging and rewarding time, 46; definition of, 25; as period of development, 43, 47, 59, 63; significance of, 53; as space of exploration, 61, 62, 166

Bildungsroman: vs. the Backfisch novel, 44; development in, 9; female, 113; vs. female coming-of-age novel, 105; and the German nation, 118–19; *Heidis Lehr- und Wanderjahre* (Spyri) and, 36; *Jane Eyre* (Brontë) and, 9; *Wilhelm Meisters Lehrjahre* (Goethe) and, 9

Bismarck, Otto von: "Blut und Eisen" speech, 119, 123–24, 125–26, 132; liberal thought vs. practical action, 131–32; nationalism and, 119, 127

Black girls' fiction, 10

"Blood and Iron." *See* Bismarck, Otto von

"Blut und Eisen." *See* Bismarck, Otto von

Bodewig, Paula, 97, 98, 103, 112

Index

borders: crossing, 125, 133–35; (de)constructing, 133–39; national identity and, 119, 124
Butler, Judith, 99, 176n2

Canfield, Dorothy, 3, 19
Chaos, The (Hopkinson), 10, 167–68
Collins, Patricia Hill, 68–69, 72
community: benefits of, 38, 116, 144, 148; benefits to, 25; borders and, 133–35; building, 123, 132, 163; creation of, 146; education and, 53; female, 66, 88, 121; gendered, 67, 105, 118, 166; healthy, 61, 105; identity of, 122; integrity of, 85; membership in, 90; mothering in, 57, 81, 89; national, 118–20, 125, 138; orphan girl and, 11; protected, 60; social fabric of, 108; successful participation in, 77; transformation of, 12, 17, 24, 141, 155, 157, 161
Comparative Children's Literature (O'Sullivan), 17, 172n14, 175n5
conversion narrative: the Backfisch book and, 96; individual effort and, 114–15; as template for spiritual development, 113; *The Wide, Wide World* as, 101. See also *Wandlungsgeschichte*
Coolidge, Susan, 32–33, 34, 53, 119, 120, 125. See also *What Katy Did: A Story*

Dagobert Claudius (character), 49, 50, 51, 52, 53, 128–30. See also *Little Moorland Princess, The*
Daisy Chain, The (Yonge), 4, 53, 156
Darwin, Charles, 93, 95
Davis, Georgiann, 99–100, 113
Davis, Lennard, 103–5, 113
DeLuzio, Crista, 24, 174n1
Disciplining Girls (Sanders), 122
domestic labor: and caring for others, 81; conversion narrative and, 95; and gender performance, 101–2, 110–11, 112–14; great social household and, 119; hidden nature of, 98; as recipe for womanhood, 114; as source of growth, 78; and the spiritual, 111
"Domesticated Romance and Capitalist Enterprise" (Tatlock), 20, 21
Duane, Anna Mae, 10, 12

Ehrenpreis, David, 118, 122
Ellen Montgomery (character): Christian conversion of, 96–97, 114; God's image and, 103; as model of female Bildungsroman, 113; spiritual maturation of, 101, 108–9; spiritual vulnerability of, 102; work of maturation and, 98–99. See also *Wide, Wide World, The*
Elsie Dinsmore (Finley), 8
Entstehung eines Backfishes aus einem Backfisch (lithograph), 94–95

fairy tales: interpretation of, 7, 66; vs. reality, 130–32
Faith Gartney (character): domestic labor and, 111–12, 115–16; education of, 102; finding community and, 77–78; and "good times," 77; independence and, 107; othermothering and, 75–76, 79–80, 81; work of maturation and, 98–99. See also *Faith Gartney's Girlhood*
Faith Gartney's Girlhood (Whitney): adult imagination in, 26; author as mentor in, 69; as Backfisch book, 53; development in, 97–98, 102, 156; double heroine in, 34; models of women in, 78–79; moral growth in, 71; spinsters in, 79; as "Sunday-school book," 34; women's financial independence in, 79–80
Faith Gartneys Mädchenjahre (*Faith Gartney's Girlhood*) (Whitney), 175n1 (ch2)

family story, 8–9, 151, 153–54
Female Adolescence in American Scientific Thought, 1830–1930 (DeLuzio), 24, 174n1
Fielding, Sarah, 7, 66
Finley, Martha, 8
Flower of the Family, The: A Book for Girls (*Die Perle der Familie*) (Prentiss): development in, 32–33, 156; homesickness and, 147, 150; identity formation in, 44, 53–56, 68; nostalgia and, 142; othermothering in, 81; the problem of female adolescence and, 56; relationships among women in, 65, 72–75; time frame in, 10
"Freche Mädchen, Freche Bücher," 12

gender: accountability, 104–5; acquisition of, 114–15; binaries, 4, 38; community and, 105, 118; construction of, 100; "doing gender," 7, 99–100, 113–14; domestic labor and, 110; feminism and, 173n22; ideologies and, 100, 143; learning restraint and, 67; national values and, 119–20; norms of, 17; performing, 110–17, 176n2; social policing of, 100; as structure, 16, 99–102, 104, 143; template for, 26; theory, 95–96
"German Women Writers and the North American Market" (Tatlock), 20
Germany and the US: connections between, 18–21; English translation of German books, 173n19; girls' books and, 118–39; women's education in, 173n22
Gettysburg Address (Lincoln): nationalism in, 119, 123, 125, 133, 139; suffering as mark of success in, 126
girls' book: adolescence and, 22, 27, 42; categories of, 7–8; characteristics of, 9–10; closure in, 79; community and, 142, 161; comparative study of, 17–22, 172n14; as conversion narrative, 114–15; development of, 7–10, 12; educational focus of, 7; genre of, 155–57, 162–63, 165; homesickness and, 143; idealization of girlhood in, 143; marriage and, 79; mentoring in, 97; narrative pattern in, 90; nationalism in, 118–20; nostalgia and, 143; origins of, 5; sentimental model in, 144; socialization in, 95; spinsters in, 73; as subgenre, 10–12; task of, 70; transformation of adults in, 74; as transgressive, 16–17; types of, 156; whiteness and, 6–7
girls' fiction. *See* girls' book
Glenn, Evelyn Nakano, 68–69
Goerth, Albrecht, 16
Good Girls, Good Germans (Askey), 120
Governess, The: or, The Little Female Academy (Fielding): as moral tale, 7; storytelling in, 66–67, 89
great social household, 119–23
Grenz, Dagmar, 16, 99
Gretchen (character): address to the reader by, 69–71; development of, 44–47, 98–99; domestic labor and, 110–11, 121; education of, 77, 101–2, 108–9; homesickness and, 106–7, 145–47; independence and, 107; othermothering and, 65, 75–77, 81; suppression of emotion and, 115–16. *See also Backfischen's Leiden und Freuden*
Gretchen's Joys and Sorrows: community of women in, 121–22; domestic metaphor in, 112; as exemplar of Backfisch book, 27, 29, 145–46; gender theory and, 95; gendered plot in, 101; impact of girls on society in, 121; othermothering in, 69–71; self-centered womanhood in, 121. *See also Backfischen's Leiden und Freuden*
Gubar, Marah, 61, 90, 141

Hall, G. Stanley: on adolescence, 22, 23, 24, 25; adolescence as problem, 63; adolescent girl's sexuality, 60; "budding girl," 18, 41–42, 59; use of *backfisch*, 43
Hamilton, Virginia, 166. See also *Sweet Whispers, Brother Rush*
Heideprinzeßchen (Marlitt, ed. Otto), 30, 175n4
Heideprinzeßchen, Das (*The Little Moorland Princess*) (Marlitt), 29–30, 44, 47–53; links to nation-building in, 124
Heidi (character): as Backfisch heroine, 157–58; community transformation and, 161; development of, 157–63; vs. Katy Carr, 161; as sentimental heroine, 158; suffering of, 160. See also *Heidis Lehr- und Wanderjahre*
Heidis Lehr- und Wanderjahre (*Heidi: Her Years of Wandering and Learning*) (Spyri), 154–63; influence of, 157; sentimental novel and, 172n14; as transitional novel, 29, 34–36, 142
Helm, Clementine, 27, 43–47, 68–70. See also *Backfischen's Leiden und Freuden*
heterosexuality: marriage, 68, 122; models of power, 68; romance, 64, 65–67, 79, 90, 161
homesick heroine, 141–63
Hopkinson, Nalo, 167–68. See also *Chaos, The*
household, great social, 119–23
Hutcheon, Linda, 145

identity: adolescence as a category of, 11; Backfisch book and, 15–16, 25, 103, 118, 165–66; Christian, 114; communal nature of, 69; development of, 42–44, 65–66, 79, 95; mature, 36, 38, 63, 112; national, 29, 118–19, 122, 125–39; racial, 6, 10; search for identity in the girls' book and, 62; women's and national identity, 129–30
Ilse (character): carelessness of, 85; education of, 87–90; obstinacy of, 26; othermothering and, 81, 84–86; self-control and, 148. See also *Obstinate Maid, An*
Ireland, Mary, 86–87

Jane Eyre (Brontë), 9, 52, 90

Katy Carr (character): border crossing and, 125, 133–35; growth through pain and, 125; healing of, 128–29; vs. Heidi, 161; homesickness and, 148; as idealized maternal figure, 135; impact of behavior and, 120; pain and authority of, 127; pain as education for, 125–26; social difference and, 138. See also *What Katy Did: A Story*

Lenore von Sassen (character): appearance of, 49–51; choices and, 49–50; development of, 47–53, 61; education and, 128–29; education of, 51–52; fairy tales and, 130–32; homesickness and, 147; Jewish identity of, 136; as member of German community, 135–36, 138; mentoring of, 49; nation-building and, 124, 126, as natural child, 47–48; preservation of identity and, 129–30; self-control and, 148; whiteness and, 136–38. See also *Heideprinzeßchen, Das*
Lincoln, Abraham, 118, 119, 125, 126, 127
Little Moorland Princess, The (Marlitt): Backfisch book and, 29–30, 44; community and, 129–30; development in, 47–53; fairy tales in, 130–32; national identity and, 119, 124, 125–26, 139; publication history of, 174n24; whiteness in, 135–38. See also *Heideprinzeßchen, Das*

Little Women (Alcott): as family story, 4, 8, 53, 156; homesickness in, 151–52; as model book, 172n14; restraint in, 46
Lucy Grant (character): development of, 32–33, 54–56; home vs. the city, 150; homesickness and, 147; identity formation and, 150; as othermother, 81; othermothering of, 72–75; relationship with God, 73, 74, 76. See also *Flower of the Family, The: A Book for Girls*

MacLeod, Anne Scott, 22, 120, 143
Mädchenliteratur der Kaiserzeit (Wilkending), 25, 120
Marlitt, Eugenie, 29, 44, 47–53, 119, 122, 124. See also *Heideprinzeßchen, Das*
maturation: anxiety of, 27, 96–99; challenges of, 38; development and, 16; education and, 53, 103–4; hard work of, 95; labor and, 36; process of, 62, 64, 80; spiritual, 101–2
McCall, Guadalupe Garcia, 166–67. See also *Under the Mesquite*
McQuillan, Julia, 99
meaning, making from suffering, 125–29
mentoring: adolescent girl and, 26, 44, 63, 86, 97, 112; by Backfisch, 62; Backfisch and, 101; choice of mentor, 48–51; civilizing effect of, 157; community, 68, 108, 144; education, and, 146; female, 11; God as mentor, 73; importance of, 62; lover as mentor, 84; narrators as mentors, 69–71; othermothers as mentors, 71–80, 91, 158, 162; peer, 66; structures for, 165–66; successful, 4, 89; whiteness and, 137
Miss in Her Teens, A, 29. See also *Backfischens Leiden und Freuden*
Miss Prigott (character), 65, 72–74, 76. See also *Flower of the Family, The: A Book for Girls*
Mitchell, Sally, 22, 60–61

Montgomery, L. M., 90. See also *Anne of Green Gables*
mothering: adolescent girl and, 80–81, 91; communal nature of, 67; difference and, 135; feminist perspective on, 67–68; models of, 68; poverty and, 80; role of book in, 70–71; romance as, 64, 74, 80–81; as shared enterprise, 75

Nodelman, Perry, 156, 172n14
nostalgia: error and, 148; homesickness and, 142–45, 150, 154, 162; for ideal past, 58

Obstinate Maid, An (von Rhoden), 30–32, 86; alienated adolescence in, 26; Christian language in, 86–87; development in, 34; the girl reader and, 89; interpretation in, 85; nostalgia in, 148–50. See also *Trotzkopf, Der: Eine Pensionsgeschichte für Junge Mädchen*
Old-Fashioned Girl, An (Alcott): as Backfisch book, 33–34, 44, 53, 56–60; development in, 156; success of, 27
Origin of Species, The (Darwin), 93
orphan girl novel: adolescence and, 11; age of girl in, 172n14; *Anne of Green Gables* as, 42; Backfisch book and, 12, 122, 141, 169; *Heidi* and, 155–57, 161–62; homesickness in, 152
O'Sullivan, Emer, 17, 175n5
othermother, the, 65–91; adolescent girl as, 80–84, 90; as independent woman, 76; love and, 74; mentors as, 71–79; narrators and, 69–71; peer, 70; romance and, 65–91; as single woman, 71–72; space of exploration and, 91; story as, 84–89; women authors as, 175n3 (ch2)

othermothering: Black feminist concept of, 36; concept of, 68; female adolescence and, 91; functions of, 69; God and, 86–87; persistence of themes of, 84; romance of, 65–91; storytelling and, 89
Our Nig (Wilson), 8

Parker, Theodore, 20
patriarchy: family structure in, 66; femininity and, 172; orphan girl novels and, 122; systems of, 4, 68, 122, 144
perfection: Backfisch book and, 53; effortlessness, illusion of, 96–99, 105, 108; questioning of, 94; whiteness and, 137
Perle der Familie, Die. See *Flower of the Family, The: A Book for Girls*
plot: Backfisch book and, 15, 49, 65; conversion narrative and, 96, 115; courtship in, 59; departure from home in, 68, 72; device, disability as, 104; device, husband as, 84; gendered, 26, 99–102; homesickness and, 158; marriage in, 47; need for education in, 29; romance and, 103; vs. sentimental novel, 80; structure of, 11, 91
Polly (character), 56–61; adolescence as opportunity, 63; as agent of transformation, 60; as Backfisch, 34; character of, 59; community and, 61; education of, 57–59; idealized girlhood of, 58; physical appearance of, 56–57; romances of, 59–60. See also *Old-Fashioned Girl, An*
Pollyanna (Porter), 4, 95, 146, 152, 156
Prentiss, Elizabeth: Germany, connection to, 19; *Stepping Heavenward*, 10; "Sunday-school books" and, 34. See also *Flower of the Family, The: A Book for Girls*

Princess of the Moor, The, 29, 174n24. See also *Heideprinzeßchen, Das*; *Little Moorland Princess, The*

Quay, Sarah, 142–43

Rebecca of Sunnybrook Farm (Wiggin), 54, 73, 74, 117–18, 143
Richardson, Samuel, 8, 9, 172n6
Risman, Barbara, 99–100, 113, 176n2
Rodgers, Beth, 22, 24, 171n14
romance: fairy tales and, 131, 132; girls' sexuality and, 61; gothic, 9, 131; heterosexual, 65–67, 79, 90, 103, 135, 161; of liberalism, 132; mothering and, 64, 65–91; nurture and, 75; othermothering and, 90; spiritual, 67, 90; whiteness and, 136
Rousseau, Jean-Jacques, 23, 25

Sanders, Joe Sutliff, 11, 122, 156, 172n14
"Sassy Girls, Sassy Books." See "Freche Mädchen, Freche Bücher"
Schmidt, Fr., 93–95
Secret Garden, The (Burnett), 9
sentimental novel, the: vs. the Backfisch book, 85, 141; emotion in, 71; vs. *Faith Gartney's Girlhood*, 80; vs. *The Flower of the Family*, 32; gendered plot in, 100–103; vs. German girls' book, 155; heterosexual romance in, 66, 84; homesickness in, 150; *The Little Moorland Princess* and, 72, 73, 74; nostalgia in, 143; orphan girl novel and, 8, 157, 158, 162; spirituality in, 105–7, 115; tropes of, 38; *The Wide, Wide World* and, 80, 96; work in, 112
Smith-Rosenberg, Carroll, 72, 80
spirituality: conversion narrative and, 113; development of, 96, 115, 162; vs. domesticity, 61, 73, 105–12; growth

of, 161; identity and, 62; maturation and, 101; vs. mentoring, 97; romance and, 67
Spyri, Johanna (*Heidis Lehr- und Wanderjahre*), 29, 34–36, 155–61, 172n14, 174n28, 177n2
Steinroetter, Vanessa, 10, 172n8
Stepping Heavenward (Prentiss), 10
suffering and making meaning, 125–29
Sweet Whispers, Brother Rush (Hamilton), 11, 166–67

Taming a Tomboy. See *Trotzkopf, Der: Eine Pensionsgeschichte für Junge Mädchen* (von Rhoden)
Tatlock, Lynne, 20, 21, 173n19
Tompkins, Jane, 95, 107
transformation, 93–116; adolescent, 24, 118, 123, 125, 138; of adults, 74; Backfisch book and, 44, 53; *Bildung* and, 176n4; community and, 155; emotional, 66; feminine, 50–51; free space for, 38; girl as agent of, 60; personal, 165; self-, 17, 61–62, 126, 128, 158; sexual, 55; successful, 47
transformation tale. See *Wandlungsgeschichte*
Trites, Roberta Seelinger, 18, 175n2
Trotzkopf, Der: Eine Pensionsgeschichte für Junge Mädchen (*An Obstinate Maid*; *Taming a Tomboy*) (von Rhoden), 30–32, 85–87

Umkehrgeschichte. See *Wandlungsgeschichte*
Under the Mesquite (McCall), 10, 166, 167
Understood Betsy (Canfield), 3, 19, 38

Vallone, Lynne, 22
von Rhoden, Emmy, 29, 30–32, 68, 84, 148. See also *Trotzkopf, Der: Eine Pensionsgeschichte für Junge Mädchen*

Wandlungsgeschichte, 15, 43
Warner, Susan, 8, 20, 95–97, 114. See also *Wide, Wide World, The*
West, Candace, 99, 100, 176n2
What Katy Did: A Story (Coolidge): as Backfisch book, 53, 128; development in, 34; nationalism and, 119, 138–39
What Katy Did at School (Coolidge), 147–48
Whitney, A. D. T., 32, 34, 53, 68, 95, 102. See also *Faith Gartney's Girlhood*
Wide, Wide World, The (Warner): Backfisch book and, 95–96; Christian education in, 96–97; editions of, 176n1; gendered plot in, 101–2; German translation of, 20; homesickness and nostalgia in, 142; as sentimental novel, 8, 85, 155; spinsters in, 73
Wiggin, Kate Douglas, 117
Wilhelm Meisters Lehrjahre (Goethe), 9, 177n2
Wilkending, Gisela, 15, 16, 25, 120
Wilson, Harriet, 8
Wright, Nazera Sadiq, 6–7, 10, 172n8

Yonge, Charlotte, 4, 13, 53
Yuval-Davis, Nira, 133

Zimmerman, Don, 99, 100, 176n2

About the Author

Photo by Sharon Meador

Julie Pfeiffer is professor of English at Hollins University, where she teaches courses on children's literature, the nineteenth-century novel, Milton, and gender and women's studies. She is the editor of *Children's Literature*, the annual of the Children's Literature Association. Her work has appeared in *Children's Literature, Mosaic, Brontë Studies, Tulsa Studies in Women's Literature,* and in edited collections.